FIND ME HAPPY

FIND ME HAPPY

A.K. PHILIPS

Matador
9 Priory Business Park,
Wistow Road, Kibworth Beauchamp,
Leicestershire. LE8 0RX
Tel: (+44) 116 279 2299
Fax: (+44) 116 279 2277
Email: books@troubador.co.uk
Web: www.troubador.co.uk/matador

ISBN 978 1780881 690

British Library Cataloguing in Publication Data.
A catalogue record for this book is available from the British Library.

Typeset in 11pt Bembo by Troubador Publishing Ltd, Leicester, UK

Matador is an imprint of Troubador Publishing Ltd

To my beautiful wife, without you this would never have happened.
Thank you for all that you have given me, I love you millions.

To my kids, you amaze me constantly and I promise to work hard
every day to show you how much I love you.

To my parents, my sisters and my brother. I love you all and feel
privileged to have you as my own.

INTRODUCTION

Welcome to *Find Me Happy*, a short book about understanding happiness and ultimately finding our own. Thank you for taking the time to read this book. I know you could be spending this time doing a multitude of other things, but I truly believe that by the time you finish this book you will feel that your time has been spent productively. The message that this book offers is universal and my biggest wish in writing this book is that you give yourself a chance to try out the one thing that this book revolves around: feeling love for yourself. If you do nothing else with yourself other than loving yourself, then I feel you'll be happier because of it!

In a world made up of societies who limp from one social problem to the next, this book is as much about understanding the world at large as it is about understanding your own life. Hopefully this book will help you gain clarity, not only on where you might want to fit in, but also on why the world looks like it does today and where it is going. When I started writing this book a few years ago the world seemed to be riding on the crest of a wave. Today it appears that the wave was indeed a tsunami.

This book is designed primarily, although not exclusively, for those of us who feel we are not as happy as we could be, people who would simply like a little more happiness in their lives. If you are content with your life as it stands and do not feel the need to make any changes at all, then I respectfully ask that you leave this book for another time, as it might not immediately serve you any benefit. With all my heart I think this book can become a tool capable of slowly changing the way we view ourselves, both individually and as a society, gradually clearing away the obstacles which restrict our happiness, but I expect some people to have a tougher journey than others. If you feel something beyond simple sadness, please talk to someone trained to assist with depression instead of trying to take it all on yourself. Believe me; it helps more than you might think. Finally, if your faith in your religion or your God is something that defines you, this is not the book for you.

My own personal journey has led me to read a lot of works, varying in their purpose, motivation and consistency, and that in turn has altered my approach to each book I have subsequently read. These stories have led me to ask challenging questions about my own existence and future, and this approach has been a consistent theme throughout my life. My ongoing journey has led me to record my thoughts in the form of this book, in the hope that I can perhaps give anyone who requires it, a little assistance in their quest for a happier life.

I could only guess as to what might have brought you to read this book, but I trust that whatever you find within these pages helps you a little on your own journey. In part, I suppose, I hope my writing ability does justice to the theory I am trying to explain. More importantly however, I hope that my theory stands true as a positive and useful tool that will enable you to make more sense of the world around you, helping you to gain a little bit more control of your own existence and ultimately help you to become happier.

The concept I am introducing is very straightforward, yet immensely complicated. I feel that this paradoxical quality has encouraged society to consistently overlook something which has been in front of it all this time. I should also mention at this point that this is a factor which has made this book so difficult to write. When you explain something simple to a person, they don't have to spend much time thinking about it to understand it. As a result of this they don't invest much energy thinking about it and the theory often slips out of their short term memory quickly. With this in mind, I will do my best to keep it as interesting and uncomplicated as possible to allow you to take from it what you so desire. I do, however, ask you to bear this in mind at all times. Although I am trying to create the best possible tool I can, this is a personal journey that will benefit you in relation to the effort you put in.

This book, although I have grown to dislike the genre, is a self help book. It is a self help book in its basest of forms. It is not about giving you a new set of rules from where you can change your life. In fact, I hope to explain why such works are usually self defeating. The only rules that truly count are the ones you actively choose to live by. There are far too many rules out there which distract us from being. This book is about reassessing the rules by which we live and choosing which we want to keep and which we want to throw away. It is about taking responsibility for our own lives and moving away from the distractions which limit our growth. It asks us to look at our understanding of the world we live in and it encourages us to re-engage with our own rules and live safely and successfully within them. We can do this through *being*.

Throughout this book I have tried to explain my journey and how this has led me to think the way I do. This should allow you to understand my true motivation for producing this book. The contents might dig the foundations of your own belief system, questioning intangible concepts like God, religion and love, but this is only a side effect of what I am trying to achieve. I understand that this can make some people initially feel uncomfortable and even angry but this is the exact opposite of what this book aims for. Therefore I ask that while reading this book you allow yourself to suspend some of your beliefs without feeling vulnerable.

I also hope that this book does not become too wordy at times! My intention is to make everything as accessible as possible. My overall approach is simple. Firstly, I will explain my whole theory in its basest form in the opening chapter. As I mentioned earlier, this might make everything seem a little anti-climactic, as what I am suggesting is very simple. In the chapters that follow, I will try to explain my view of the world and how I came to see things as I do now. As each individual chapter progresses, you might find that you need to take each paragraph slowly in order to fully grasp what I am saying.

In the third section, I will suggest a few exercises that helped me along the process. Again, this is not about applying new rules for you to live by in order to make use of my theory. It is more about 'creating a habit' that will become a first step in feeling love for yourself. It is about getting a bit of quiet time for yourself in order to start appreciating the happiness that lies within you, and it is about allowing yourself to make up your own rules at your own speed. It has taken me a long time to get to where I am, and I still have a whole life of discovery ahead of me, so don't expect to understand or feel everything on the first go. Don't get stressed if you initially struggle to understand something I am trying to convey, but equally I ask that you don't dismiss it. Take your time and live your life, and if you feel it's getting too much, come back to the book when you feel you are ready to do so. The theory is simple but becomes complicated as you begin to live it. Once you grasp the fundamentals it will then become simple once more.

To end this relatively short book I aim to take a quick look at the world around us and identify the challenges I believe this theory relates to. I don't want to get ahead of myself, but I do think that by simply making a small adjustment to how we see ourselves, we can have a big impact on our happiness and how we view the world around us.

I am neither a guru nor a genius, a poet nor a scientist. I don't think you will find anything in the words that follow that has not been written before. Indeed, this work is a collection of things I have perceived due to the life I have lived, lessons I have learned and the books I have read. The only true piece of originality I strive for is the simple compilation and re-ordering of things that we already know. To do this I aim to dispel the idea of leaps of faith, and the complicated and often hopeful conclusions which have been the shortfall of so many great theories. This book is about stripping away 'secret of life' or external theories, allowing you to look at what we know as opposed to what we are hoping to find. It is, in its essence, about starting from a new beginning.

One thing that will become noticeable is the generalisations I use to help explain everything. I was brought up in a predominantly Christian society and this dictates some of the terms used. I sincerely hope that those of you who originate from non Christian societies forgive these generalisations, and I apologise to all people of faith if they find anything here offensive. Part of my theory, as I alluded to earlier, involves questioning the purpose and existence of many beliefs, including God's, prophets, deities and religion in general. I am not trying to be divisive and I ask for a little room to manoeuvre in order to fully explain myself. If at this stage you feel that such a journey is not for you, then I gladly embrace your decision. Indeed, if you want you can send me back the book with your receipt and I will give you a refund.

Part of my theory requires the removal of political, personal and manmade influences of what God has become. This allows us to look at the original carnation of God before his or her name was used for the advancement of any one individual. In truth, I believe that in doing this we are free to re-engage with our own God if that is indeed our desire. It should also be pointed out that one of my core beliefs is that the earth is hundreds of millions of years old and society has evolved over at least 70,000 years, and that mankind existed before religion.

To conclude, I would like to thank every single person who has been part of my life. Some of you have inspired me in spite of your actions, some because of them. I have a very solid basis to my life, and that has allowed me to recover from both my mistakes and my own personal issues. Furthermore there are quite a few individuals (and you all have at least a small inkling who you are) who have been key to this book. I probably haven't fully explained to you how grateful I really am, but hopefully the contents of this book will go some way to show it.

Thanks again and keep smiling.

WHERE DO I START?

The world can be a wonderful place. Sometimes it is a place where people help each other, experiences are shared and laughter fills the air. Sometimes it is a place where the sun shines enough to make us feel happy but not so much that it causes droughts. When my world is like this, there is nowhere I would rather be. Unfortunately the world isn't always like this. My world has poverty, famine, violence, greed and one-upmanship to distract from all the beautiful things that exist. My world changes everyday, ebbing and flowing, usually promising of hope, sometimes hinting at despair. Yet despite of everything, my world always has the potential to be beautiful.

With mankind evolving every day into something which is less than what we had hoped for and more what we hope to change, it is becoming easier to notice the lack of happiness in society. Some people feel sad that the sun has gone and that there is poverty and inequality. Others feel sad because they have less than they want or because they feel they are worth less than others, materially or otherwise. Societies come together to react against institutions, and governments react to maintain their authority. Some people are sad about things that *are*, whilst others are sad with what they *perceive*. Regardless of the sadness that exists around you, it is more about how you deal with sadness that defines your relationship with happiness.

Sadness has its place in life, but it should not be a constant companion. Feeling sad for a reason is part and parcel of life, but feeling sad as a general state is something different. Sadness should be a lighthouse to warn us as much from shallow waters as from the jagged rocks, a signal that nudges us when we are in danger of doing ourselves ' real damage. Perhaps sadness is not so much a state of mind as a warning that we are far enough removed from happiness to want to make a change to our direction. If this is indeed the case, then what is happiness?

What do you see when you step back and try to examine your own world? For me it depends upon three main things: my mood, my recent experiences and my environment. If I am in a positive mood, my day has been good and I am in a safe place with people I feel comfortable, then the world is far more likely to be good. It is easier to see a beauty in everything. The flowers appear brighter, smiles are fuller and more plentiful, and more good stuff seems to happen. If, however, I have had a tough day, with no one I like around me, I am more vulnerable to the negativities of our world. People seem more impatient, at times even aggressive. I often don't notice the flowers and a feeling of uneasiness in my stomach is never far away.

I think a lot of people can relate to this, whilst many more might well be unaware of it. We are individuals after all. Each of us have different ways of looking at and experiencing the world, yet there is one significant commonality of process held by nearly all of us. We can look at the exact same scenario many times, and depending upon our specific state of mind and our general personality, we can interpret things with wildly contrasting conclusions.

What I mean is simple. Imagine you are having a picnic in a busy park and a ball bounces over to you and spills a small amount of your drink. If you are feeling happy, you are *more likely* to wave off the occurrence without any stress. If, however, you are in a bad mood, you might find the situation causes you some stress or even anger.

This happens because our brain subconsciously runs through a multitude of processes based upon the relative experiences or knowledge we have already had, analysing the scenario and readying a range of possible reactions in case they are needed. As this is a subconscious action, we are generally not aware of the process. It only becomes significant if we feel a change in our general level of awareness which tells us to get ready to act.

Let's take a different scenario. You are in a public place which is new to you, a coffee shop or a pub for example. There is a small crowd of people in the corner making a lot of noise. A man from that group walks past and looks straight at you without smiling. He looks at your drink, your coat which is sitting beside you, slowing his pace before going past you into the toilet. How do you feel?

We will all feel slightly different, so instead of suggesting how you are feeling I will explore what is happening in your head. There are two main factors to be aware of. Firstly, because of how our brain works, our subconscious runs through the archives of our memory to access emotions, memories and judgements which correlate to this specific event. Have we been in this environment before? Have we any memories of events which are similar to this? Basically, what experiences do we have that might possibly be connected? The second point of note is that there is a part of our internal makeup influencing these automatic actions. This part is our inner voice and it affects the angle from which our subconscious approaches our internal appraisal of the event.

We all have this inner voice. This is something I will expand upon later, however at this point in time I will just introduce it. It is a part of ourselves which for some is very loud and for others quite quiet. It is that voice inside of us that we hear when we are thinking. Some voices are strong and opinionated, others are passive. It is the voice of our subconscious and it speaks from a point relative to how we see ourselves inside. If we genuinely feel happy, the voice will generally aim to put a positive spin on the things we come across in our everyday life. If we have developed a poor opinion of ourselves, then this voice will use this opinion to put a negative spin on things when the opportunity arises.

As well as having a *general* level of positivity or negativity, we also have a *present* state of positivity or negativity, something which reflects our *present* mood due to current events in our life. If we are *generally* in a negative state of mind, *general* observations we have will be interpreted with a negative spin, making it more likely that we will have a negative *present* state of mind. If we have a negative *present* state of mind we will automatically be drawn to the negative aspects in specific events.

Getting back to the scenario, in the public place with the stranger passing, we will split all possible reactions into four groups. Group one are positive people who are in a positive mood, group two are positive people who are in a negative mood, group three are negative people who are in a positive mood and finally group four are negative people who are in a negative mood. Generally, the people

5

from group one would not even be sufficiently aware of the scenario to react, while the people from the second group would be aware but not think too much about it. People from the third group would feel vulnerable but try to think their way out of it and the people in group four would feel both vulnerable and anxious and may be brought to react in some way. They may change seats, leave, or create a confrontational environment.

One of the most important events in my life was the moment I began to fully appreciate that everyone sees the world differently. People look at the world relative to their own experiences, to their general happiness and their specific happiness. I had always been aware of this but I had never really explored the idea. When I did take it on board it meant a great deal to me, as up until that point I had been someone who generally didn't feel happy with their lot.

This change of viewpoint allowed me to realise that if I was genuinely happy then I would be less affected by the world around me, and if I was genuinely unhappy I would always tend to find ways of interpreting events from a negative perspective. It allowed me to see that *what happens in the world around me is only ever secondary to what my general state of mind is, as it is this state that directs my interpretation of the world.* This was also the state of the voice inside me. It was probably the most significant discovery of my life.

This realisation slowly conspired to create a new found strength within me. At the time when I started this journey, I was generally someone who felt quite a bit of sadness intermittently sprinkled with moments of happiness, but ultimately I was unhappy and never thought life would get much better. When I understood that it was my inner state which dictated my overall feelings, I made myself a promise to find and understand a true and lasting happiness. After all, I didn't have that much to lose!

For the next few years, I endeavoured to understand happiness. I never knew what true happiness was or where to look for it, but I was sure I would know it when I found it. I also knew I would find it eventually. I was convinced that it had to exist, therefore I was one hundred percent certain I would find it, regardless of its guise. In my life before this, experience had told me what it wasn't, but I really couldn't for the life of me figure out what it was. I researched philosophies and religions and studied strategies and theories, yet none of them could stand up under lengthy examination. I embraced various ways of living, believing that one day I would work out a successful model for life whereby mankind could move away from the negativities of society. Then, on a day when I wasn't particularly seeking it, the penny dropped.

I had taken a long time to get to that point, the point where it all fitted perfectly into place, but I can honestly say the answer was there all along. It wasn't written in code in an ancient book, there was no secret or hidden civilisation, nor was there a conspiracy theory involving lizards. One morning, after a particularly good sleep, everything made sense.

In the last three years, I have tried every day to live by the theory which presented itself on that morning, sometimes challenging it, looking for anything I might have missed. I am constantly surprised with the simplicity of the conclusion I arrived at. Most days, my inner state becomes a tiny bit happier and, as a result, my life has changed immensely. There is absolutely no *magic* involved. This is not something that you need to do twice a week for six months, nor is it a ten step program to achieve happiness. It is something that, once understood, will gradually become part of you.

There is a very plain reason why this whole concept appeared simple to me. It was the result of fifteen years of climbing a mountain and one second of reaching the summit. I was searching for it, living it and analysing every single aspect of my life, using my own experiences as a tool of judgement, constantly learning from what I uncovered. Since an early age, I have always challenged the laws of society in my head, as I believed that there was more to this life than which had been explained to me. As a result, I was never fully restricted by any specific belief system, religious or otherwise. Indeed, I have embraced quite a few belief systems during my life in my search for that illusive true happiness.

When everything fell into place and started to make sense, I found it very hard to elucidate my thoughts as they were so new to me. Initially I hadn't really applied my thoughts to the challenges society offered, so I could not understand the full connotations of what was becoming my core philosophy. I tried to talk to people about it, but they didn't seem as blown away as I was. In fact, when I tried to break it down for people in the hope that they would 'get it', I quickly realised that most people don't want to be told how to see the world. Nor do they want to have their own outlook of the world affected. This lesson in itself was invaluable. Not only did I understand how people felt when someone tried to convert them to a religion, I actually realised how wrong it was to try to change people's outlook on life without their expressed permission. This book should only ever serve as a resource to someone who wants assistance in understanding happiness.

The other difficulty in trying to explain how I see the world is that I am saying something that is so simple, that as a society we have for thousands of years overlooked its lessons. The reason for this is that our general understanding of the world throughout history has over-complicated life. All I hope to do is point to the manmade misconceptions and complications and let you make up your own mind.

So, let's cut to the chase, what is this simple theory that will allow me to understand happiness? Well, here it is.

LEARN TO LOVE YOURSELF.

BY EXPRESSING UNCONDITIONAL LOVE FOR OURSELVES AND FEELING FULLY ACCEPTING OF OUR OWN LOVE, WE CAN BECOME FREE FROM THE THINGS WHICH DETRACT FROM LIVING. BY FEELING LOVE FOR OURSELVES WE AUTOMATICALLY CREATE A PLACE MADE FROM HONESTY, POSITIVITY AND LOVE, FROM WHERE ALL OUR FUTURE ACTIONS ORIGINATE.

IS THAT IT?!

BY EXPRESSING UNCONDITIONAL LOVE FOR OURSELVES AND FEELING FULLY ACCEPTING OF OUR OWN LOVE, WE CAN BECOME FREE FROM THE THINGS WHICH DETRACT FROM LIVING. BY FEELING LOVE FOR OURSELVES WE AUTOMATICALLY CREATE A PLACE MADE FROM HONESTY, POSITIVITY AND LOVE, FROM WHERE ALL OUR FUTURE ACTIONS ORIGINATE.

Love yourself.

That, in a nut shell, is my theory! How do you feel? Confused, awoken, unmoved, happy? Well, as I said, it is simple but simultaneously complex, so let's expand on this a bit. If I was to ask you to mark on a scale of 1 to 10 how happy you feel when you feel full of love, what would your mark be? And what about when you felt there was no love in your life? And finally, what about now? What mark would you give yourself at this very moment?

Now, try to visualise yourself in each of the above states, full of love, void of love and at this actual moment, whilst imagining you spilled something hard to shift on a favourite piece of clothing. Pay attention to your marks out of 10. Were there any changes? The reason I ask this is that as someone who can be a little clumsy, I have often spilled food and drink over myself! If I spilled something on myself when I was in a loved up state, happy both generally and specifically, I merely laughed it off. If I did it when I was in a sad general state, even if I was specifically happy, it could knock me back a few steps.

Our general happiness is learned. It is learned in relation to our home environment and our earliest communications. It is impacted upon by the personality of our parents and our siblings and the dynamics that this creates. It evolves beside our perception of our natural abilities, the tools we have developed and our ability to utilise them both in a productive way. Although not fixed, our general happiness can be compared to a large object that requires significant force to move it, with any movement almost always being slow unless the force is extraordinary. Our specific happiness stays within the range of our general happiness but it is relative to our thoughts at that moment.

Basically, this interpretation of the world suggests that the happier we are, the happier we will be because of how we see the world, and the less content we are, the more we see unhappiness in the world. This can be the most debilitating cycle ever to someone who is unhappy and even more so to someone who is depressed. This understanding in itself is eye opening. If being happy helps us stay happy and being sad conspires to keep us sad, all we need to do is understand our inner state and how to make it happy. Be happy to be happy.

When I began my search for true happiness, I did so with two beliefs: one, that true happiness existed, and two, I would find it. I read a lot, studying books on Christianity, Islam, and Judaism. I looked at Hinduism, Buddhism and general eastern philosophies. I also investigated more recently significant belief systems which seemed to offer modern day answers, like Kabbalah and Reiki. These led to quantum physics and psychology, hypnotherapy and life coaching.

Patterns started to emerge, moral ideals held constant. Don't kill, steal or covet. Live pure, love your family and be humble. Live a good life and serve a higher being or energy, show and feel gratitude every day. As I read and lived through each belief system, I often felt inspired by what they said, believing each time that this might be my way to find happiness. Yet every time I would reach a point where cracks would start to appear in the consistency of the philosophy or religion. These cracks too seemed to have patterns.

I had exhausted most of my avenues to find happiness because one of two (or both) things happened. Either fundamental elements that were supposedly cast in stone where found to be easily disproved or I was expected to make enormous leaps of faith that went against my concept of common sense. I seemed to continually get close to finding a path towards happiness only to find a problem at the last minute.

Due to the fact I was running out of directions to look, I decided to re-examine my understanding of history and try to understand how we got to where we are today, hoping to spot something I had never seen before. You see, at this stage I was becoming more and more disaffected by certain aspects of the world and I wanted to fix it. Greed, poverty, violence and war, drugs, sickness, genocide, addictions and murder had all become common every day stories . If I could find the key to true happiness, I could share my discovery with the world and make it a happier place. And if the world was happy, then at last I would be too. Was this a noble thought or simply the hopes of a desperate man?

I took a look at where we stand today, both as individuals and as a society, and how we arrived here. I surmised that w*e are where we are as a direct result of our decisions and the decisions of those who went before us.* This is true both for the individual and for the world and it gives us a starting point to work from. The question becomes, "where might we have started in order to have arrived at where we now are?"

All major societies require a model of governing to survive. Such models have two basic requirements: *a*, a framework from where the masses can work, for example a set of laws, and *b*, a focal point to preside over it. In many cases, these governing models are complimented by a moral model, designed to strengthen it. These moral models require a prophet, deity, God (or their plural equivalent), or a human who fulfils a 'deity on earth' role. We have labelled a majority of these moral models as religions. Societies that thrive without religion use philosophies which mould the moral governance required to verify their ideals.

If we go back to the earliest civilisations, using the scientifically accepted timeline, there was no religion, no accepted God(s) and no mass government. After initial evolution, there were simply small tribes of people with their own simple belief systems. As mankind evolved from its basest origins, it continually discovered new things. The continual education and evolution of the human race required them to distinguish that which was beneficial from that which was detrimental to their actual existence. In order for societies to evolve they needed a medium to pass on the lessons of their predecessors to their successors or else they would continually succumb to the same fate. They needed a form of communication to pass down vital information to the young of their tribe to ensure they could stay alive. Some of the earliest examples of this can be found in, for example, primitive cave drawings.

Continuing with this thought process; as societies evolved, so did their capacity to communicate, their wish to learn and the desire to survive. In order to stop their successors being exposed to known dangers, communication evolved and early societies created easy to follow guidelines which could be passed from generation to generation. As societies in their origins were relatively primitive, they viewed the world from a very base perspective. They could understand some of what was going on in the world around them but in general they knew very little about the laws of nature; knowledge that we now take for granted. As a result, most of these societies learned to believe that something must exist that was bigger than them, and that thing, whatever we might now call it, became deities of sorts.

The establishment of an intangible presence allowed individuals to justify events which their existing belief systems had no explanation for: floods and famines, plagues and earthquakes, sickness and punishments. Evolving societies needed to be able to make sense of these events in order to know how to react, prevent or safeguard against them. For this understanding they looked to the wiser members of their tribes. Often natural selection would dictate who led a tribe based upon physicality or bloodline, but as communication became more intricate and questions began to be raised, people called for someone to offer answers.

Most people who found themselves in such positions of influence or power lived lives of relative comfort. Such comfort or adulation, and the possible loss off, is a great motivator to drive us to further understand the world around us. Imagine someone two hundred, never mind ten thousand, years ago trying to explain an earthquake. Why did it happen, would it happen again, was there anything they could do? Many of them formulated answers which made sense to them, and these frameworks, led the way to the creation of many historical Gods.

Some of these people believed in what they were creating, whilst others realised that cultivating believable deities could assist their people to live a safe, fruitful and positive existence. Some however, dare I say it, abused their power and created or manipulated Gods to maintain and advance their own personal positions and that of their family.

As we continue along the early evolution of man, certain individuals realised that the existence of a God could assist as a method of governance, whilst others fully believed all that they had been taught in relation to the existence of Gods. It does, after all, sit perfectly with our innate self governing process of 'avoid what harms you and move towards what nourishes you'. In primitive society, if you don't keep your people in check, give them a set of rules and a reason to follow them, then the society is liable to collapse. It therefore made sense to not just formalise the position of a God or Gods into their society, but also to attribute acts of great consequence to these deities to help control growing numbers.

This method of explaining the unexplainable, whilst simultaneously governing societies, has consistently repeated itself throughout history. The majority of, if not all, major societies looked upon the lessons their life had afforded them and decided that (regardless of the specifics and ever changing face of God) mankind, both individually and collectively, was best managed by a generalised philosophy. This philosophy utilised the understanding that, as we are motivated by pain and pleasure, the existence of a God or Gods could assist, or even be, a method of controlled governance. Religions with basic Gods evolved or were crushed by religions with more complex Gods. Mankind was becoming more intelligent and simple Gods couldn't stand up to the rigours of evolving man. Simplistic religions were amalgamated into more complex ones. Norse Gods, Greek Gods, Egyptian,

Roman and most of the other ancient Gods died because they couldn't meet the new challenges they subsequently faced. The lessons that this taught, found their way into newer more complex religions.

If we were to gloss over the last thousand years and take even a basic understanding of the evolution of religions and indeed societies in general, we would see massive changes created by the need of the model to survive. Many faiths have split, creating newer versions or interpretations of earlier setups, often leading to disputes over who is right and who is wrong. Stories built upon stories designed from a two pronged need, to explain the unexplainable, whilst keeping some form of accountable order.

If today we were to remove deities or Gods from societies, many would initially struggle to find a way of providing a moral compass. Indeed, some societies have removed previously accepted God's, theologies and religions from their framework and replaced them with an alternative (invariably dictatorial) entity. As a result of such social occurrences, most societies who have looked on from the outside see this approach as a non starter. This is because they were trying to replace one set of externally verified rules with another.

On top of this, as has happened time and time again throughout history, when one faith seems to become so strong that it is challenging the legitimacy of another, elements of most God fearing societies have found ways of manipulating their own take on God's will to exterminate other God fearing societies, propagating the devil (or his cohorts) as reason enough to proliferate their one true vision of God's path.

So, where has this left us? The world and its faiths and religions have become so diverse that without some magnificent intervention from one of the accepted Gods, we are destined to eventually wipe out our species as we know it. Mind you, if this magnificent intervention does materialise, then only a few will be saved and the rest of us are doomed. For a majority of us, it has basically become a lose lose situation regardless of how it all pans out!

Or has it? This is what predicates my theory. At the various key points in time when mankind had taken it as an absolute truth that something bigger than us (a God, energy or deity) has existed from before the advent of mankind, it gradually cemented its status as an externally verifying society. Every collective society, so ingrained in its essence, has perpetuated that everything we do is judged by an external entity (this includes karma). It gave us a reason to be good and a reason not to be bad. If we were to explore a possibility whereby we remove the manmade Gods and evolved religions (just as an experiment in our own able minds) we would have to look for a reason to be morally just. What if, in all of our collective desires to be saved, positively reincarnated or live a life of eternal happiness, we overlooked a simple but cataclysmic error in judgement?

Most of us believe that love requires at least two elements to exist. We are conditioned (remember how significant religion is or has been in most societies, even in our very recent history) to believe that there is a God or an entity and that we should love that God or entity more than we should love ourselves. As a result, very few mainstream societies understand how to embrace love to its fullest. If a God exists and we are made in his image, then surely we must love ourselves first and foremost? Then again, if there is no God must we not love ourselves first before we are strong enough to be able to truly love another?

As a result of thousands of years of conditioning, such a philosophy as truly loving yourself seems alien. Even in cultures where love is promoted and we proclaim to love ourselves, it is almost impossible to do it to a successful enough level to stop us being affected by the collective path of the world we live in. Indeed, when most of us try to love ourselves, our understanding of the world we live in and the belief systems that shout loudest have put distractions like guilt in the way. When most of us try to love ourselves, a voice from within us points out our flaws. For the most part, this results in the belief we aren't actually deserving of our own love. We forget that the decisions we made in our own past were based upon a set of beliefs that weren't actually foolproof. As we continually evolve and learn, developing newer interpretations of the world and new guidelines, it is easy to forget that we would have lacked knowledge or experience in the past.

As a result of this, love has been moulded from an unconditional entity that we are all worthy of interacting with, into something that comes with a set of rules that you might not even agree with or understand. When love becomes something we seek as opposed to something we possess, our main coping mechanism is then to externalise our efforts and try to seek love from others.

It has become natural for people to judge their worth against the perception of, and the perceived worth of, others. We develop a 'rule base' through the lessons we learned as we grew up. Everyone has a different set of experiences to draw upon, therefore everyone's rules are, at best, slightly different. Even when we compare ourselves against those who are closest to us genetically, our siblings and our parents, we tend to forget that the perspective we have is dictated by what we take from our specific interactions with people, and these interactions are relative to whom they are with and where they are in their own life, as well as where we are in ours.

The possibilities afforded by our genetic makeup and

the lessons that are offered by those in a relative position to our holistic growth, conspire to create an evolving classroom. In this environment we build our understanding of the world in relation, not to the lessons offered, but to what has been gradually learned through our experiences. Not everyone learns what they are being taught because the small signifiers of experience that the teacher uses in their explanation might not exist in the student's world.

When we all work from different 'rule base's', it is natural that there will be many little rule conflicts. Some children learn to grab whilst others might learn to believe this is not allowed. To push or not to push, to want or not to want, to interact or not to interact? When many tiny differences to rule bases exist even within families, the application of a set of governing rules will automatically be limiting in its rigidity.

As a result of us not knowing any better, most of us externalise to determine where we are in life. The problem with this desire for external verification however, is that we either judge others by our own yardstick or more commonly, we try to work out the yard stick of others and then apply it to ourselves. As you might imagine, both strategies are flawed.

Obviously, there are a significant number of people who have become evil and caused widespread irrevocable pain. These are people who, for various reasons, have carried out atrocities most of us cannot even fathom. Yet most of the rest of us wrongly believe that we are either weak people or at best, not nice/attractive at times. If we are motivated by external and ever changing factors which are dependent upon the opinion of others, we will continually struggle to go in any one direction. We either do things we believe others will like in the hope that we will be loved, or give up on the society that labels us and live our life in spite of the rules and beliefs that are used to brand and judge us. Some people think that if everyone else is happy then they can start to make themselves happy. At one stage I did. Invariably however, we compare ourselves unfairly to others, leading us to find reasons to over or under value ourselves, which in turn affects our opinion on how truly deserving of love we might be.

The last few paragraphs try and explain how most of us have, to some degree, felt. There are actually people who seem to get it (my theory of truly loving ourselves) and ultimately understand happiness. Most of these people don't understand how the rest of us feel and as a result they cannot relate to us. They are the lucky ones for whom the cards have fallen kindly and often this can cause us even more consternation!

My conclusion is as follows. Most societies are conditioned through history to be externally verifying, to try to do the right thing based on an external set of beliefs.

As these beliefs are ever changing and often misguided, those of us who look to others for a lead will always be left wanting. We need to learn how to love ourselves and trust that we are in essence (or at least we can be) self verifying people. We need to forgive the mistakes we made and the perceived mistakes of others and realise that loving yourself is a lifetime vocation, and that the random nature of life will always challenge us. The more we realise that the mistakes we made where a product of our own decisions and the decisions we made were based on a belief system which wasn't as solid as we once thought, the more we can allow ourselves to become more worthy of our own forgiveness and love. The more we love ourselves, the more we will love as we become stronger within ourselves. The more we love ourselves, the less we will judge others. When we start to realise that rules are different and individual to each of us, we feel less inclined to judge. The less we judge others the easier it is to forgive ourselves and the freer we will be to love ourselves a little more.

Ultimately, we should only need external verification to ground us (I think about 15% external verification and 85% internal is a positive ratio). Every coping mechanism we previously used will be easier to adapt. We will learn not to try to teach, rather to live by example and from love, as we slowly realise that everyone else has been living their own lives governed by their own rules. If individually we become 1% happier every year, then society could very quickly regain control of its destination.

And there you have it. It's a lot to take in but I do think it will make a lot of sense the more you think about it. As you learn to love yourself, things become less complicated and you will be more able to forgive and thus grow. This cycle of loving yourself will give you a full understanding of happiness specific to how it relates to your own life. You will become happier by default.

There is very little else new in this book. The rest of the chapters are based upon breaking this down and explaining it further from a few different perspectives. Hopefully you will create your own strategy for how best to live your life and no longer feel the need to live by the rules of others. Remember, everyone's strategy will be unique. It is a personal journey that leaves judgement at the door. If I'm right, and I truly hope I am, the theory, philosophy or whatever you want to call it, will allow you to take your time to enjoy living your life and stop worrying about the judgements of others or about saving the world. Start with yourself and you'll soon become strong enough for whatever the world throws at you.

BREAKING IT ALL DOWN

So let's take a brief recap before we go any further. In the last two chapters I put forward a theory and explained how I got there. It's not a new theory; it's just never really been pulled together in this way. Have you ever listened to the words of John Lennon's 'Imagine'? You should listen to it. He asks us to imagine what it would be like if there was nothing, only us. A great song which I had listened to over one hundred times yet never truly grasped. Every part of my hypothesis has already been put forth at many stages throughout our history. Some people have spoken of loving ourselves and most religions speak of forgiveness faith and love. Philosophers have questioned religions and offered new answers. It just so happens that for some reason, one fundamental part has been overlooked. This is not my theory, it is a theory that has existed in fragments since the dawn of time, and I am only starting to truly understand it.

As you read this book I ask that you do not get too caught up in my opinion or my story. I am using a personal narrative because it should make it easier for people to understand happiness and what loving yourself first can do. How you see the world is totally relative to your life experiences and this might mean that my experiences bear no relation to your own. This is why I ask that you don't get caught up in my story, rather that you test the philosophy in a way that suits you.

I am just a happy man (who now believes he has it fully within his power to grow happier) who was at times someone who felt helpless and sad. I tried almost every avenue available to me to find an answer. I manipulated events, trying to make people like me, in an attempt to feel valued, yet as a younger man I never truly accepted the love of people who loved me for me. My self esteem never grew much in my earlier years so I never valued my own opinion, except as a tool to try to impress. I tried to work out the rules of others and pre-empt what might make them happy whilst simultaneously thinking that those closest to me would disown me if they ever knew some of the things I had done. I hadn't actually done much wrong but I did view attempts to make people happy as misleading. I figured they wouldn't have put up with me if they knew the 'real' me.

At times, I did things in spite of myself because I believed that people judged me regardless of my actions, I thought I may as well just be a lost wondering soul. I didn't value myself, so why should someone else? Why should I try to better myself? Why should I go through heartache and difficult times when I knew there was always going to be something else to knock me straight back down again every time I started to feel some happiness?

Everything I tried (self help, hypnotherapy, counselling, faking) failed to significantly improve my situation. I took the people I loved (there where a whole lot less than I thought, but I loved them a whole lot more than I knew) for granted. I wanted to escape from them, and from the me that they knew, because I didn't really like that me. One day, I was sure, they would suss me out, call my bluff and I would have nothing. As long as I kept trying to fix myself and avoid who I was, then I would never have to embrace what I might lose.

And I did escape. I took time to collect my thoughts and be someone else: a new me. I practised showing love and preaching happiness. I read the types of books that many of us have, hoping to find the answer I craved. I fully believed that I could fake it 'til I made it, but that didn't work either. However, at least I was stronger and I had forgiven myself for a few of my mistakes. I still worried about making people happy, I still hid from myself in crowded rooms and I still yearned to be fixed by some magic wand. At least I had dealt with a few of the demons from the darkest recesses of my mind and soul.

I took a good look at all I had learned, read and absorbed, and I chose an old sales mantra, 'Keep It Simple, Stupid' as my guide. I had learned rules, reasons, stories, motivation and oh so many other buzz words. One day after removing the opinions I perceived to exist, I started afresh. I took the experiences I gained in my attempts to work out what I thought people wanted me to be and I realised something. I realised that if I was trying to come up with a theory to save the world so that I would have somewhere safe to live, I would have to come up with a great story. And then I asked myself, where might this approach have been taken before?

If you were to become the ruler of your own community, how would you keep a significant number of different people sufficiently happy to allow you to be happy? There is only one way to do it. You must create a force with the right to judge the community without contest and you must be able to get a sufficient amount of significant people to buy in, in order to back up what you have created so that you can manage the masses. You either do this through brute force or the invention of a story that will give people a *raison d'être*. This was a valid explanation of the maintenance of most successful societies.

If most societies were based upon the desire of individuals to manage events to promote safety, growth and happiness of the people, then this was merely the same as what I craved. Leaders wanted a vehicle for the masses to be happy so that they could be happy and maintain their position. I wanted to find a strategy that I could show the world so that I could be happy and safe forever. It just so happens that such strategies or philosophies ultimately become victims of their own flaws, as they are both exclusive and man-made.

In taking this realisation on board I had to accept a new truth. I could no longer blame people or society for where I found myself in life. I had to stop trying to fix everyone or everything and I had to stop judging myself. I was beginning to view the world in a completely new way, but what did I now need to face up to?

The only thing that made sense to me was this: what if the messages were right but the stories were wrong? Maybe the philosophies were close, but the strategies fell short? If the irrefutable answer hadn't been found over thousands of years of modern society, in the external, the only other place left to look was inside. What if, instead of trying to create a happy world (according to my rules) in which I could live safely, I must first simply find a way to be happy with *who I really was*?

My life and experiences have culminated in a world view which makes sense to me on all levels, and as a result directs me to believe that there are fundamental flaws in society which have brought us to where we are today, in a good world containing some bad elements. I believe that the world has been conditioned to believe love is something that you give to others but not yourself, a belief system which has ingrained itself deeply into our collective subconscious due mainly to the creation and formulation of a God or Gods. I believe that this notion has led to mankind overlooking the possibility that through loving ourselves, mankind will find the redemption it so craves. I believe that if you do not have love for yourself, you have no fuel to love for any great length of time. Nor do you have an anchor to stop you getting dragged about in the sea of life.

I feel that if you truly love yourself, everything you do will come from a loving place. As a result, you won't be judgemental of others, nor will you ever do anything which will intentionally cause harm. The more you love yourself, the more you will understand love. It is unconditional, without need for boundaries or attachments. It just is, without compromise.

I believe that by learning to love myself, one day at a time, I am gradually less affected by the negativities of the world around me. As I am less affected by these negativities, I am less distracted and happier for longer periods of time. As a direct result of this, my interactions with others involve more love and less judgement, more forgiveness (of myself and others) and fewer conditions. I am grateful for what I have and I feel more inclined to be grateful for the ability to appreciate the world I live in.

I no longer feel the need to heal the world. Every day I learn a little more about love, become a little more humble and a little more loving. In my interactions I try hard to be positive no matter what events unfold in front of me, creating fewer distractions for others. Maybe by not beeping at the person who felt the need to cut me off in traffic, they might not have the reason to keep a negative cycle going. Maybe by being as courteous as I can, someone will feel a little better about humanity. Regardless of what might happen, all I can truly control is my own feelings, so by loving myself I learn how to live a life of happiness and love.

So, what about God and religion? As you might already have guessed, I believe that all religion is created by man, for man. Now that statement might make some of you feel a bit defensive of your religion, and that's fine. If you are dedicated to your religion, you will either by default believe that all other religions are totally wrong, or not think too much about it and just be content in your own beliefs. Well, for this book this is the same; you can look at my non religious beliefs in the same way as you look at other religion's apart from your own.

Although I believe all religions are purely man-made, I would never try to detract from the role it has played in the development of some of the most beautiful and influential people the world has produced. I just happen to think that all of these people, and many others who religion excluded, might have found a more personal vehicle in loving themselves first. Whilst religion has provided the world with many benefits and inspired many great people, it also has a darker side.

I think we have missed the 'truly love yourself' idea because often the biggest winners in religion are the powerful rule makers within. I believe that the problem with religion is simply that it is completely man-made. The key theories of most, if not all, religions generally espouse great and humble things, however, it is when man tries to interpret teachings for his own gain that conflict occurs.

How futile are the wars between religions and those within religions? What are these wars actually over? What are the differences between Christians and Muslims, Jews and Hindus, or Catholics and Protestants that are so great that they lead mankind to kill in the name of God? I have absolutely no problem with most religious beliefs and apologise in advance for any hurt that I have caused by suggesting that all religions have been created to explain the unexplainable and to govern, but religion has a lot to answer for.

So where does that leave God? Is there a God? For

me, no, at least not in the manufactured sense. I cannot see how a God can exist within the conflicting and suitably interpreted confines given him, her or it by the many different religions who own the copyright. I can see no bearded man in heaven or any other manifestation of a conscious God. That is just my opinion.

Still I believe that it's a possibility that perhaps, as a result of the conscious and subconscious aspirations of mankind, a force may exist that is not confined to being in the image of man, in neither its form, personality nor tendencies. Now when someone mentions God, I simply replace the man with the philosophy, love. Love does not judge. It is pure, omnipotent, never ending, forgiving, supportive, and many more things. Love is an energy so strong that it can redeem the most lost of people. Love can make the complicated seem simple, love takes every good feeling you have and makes it better. I feel that God is not love, but Love is God.

TWO BASIC GUIDELINES

There are two basic guidelines which shape my approach to life. They have become my automatic check valves, constantly working away, continuously prodding me gently in certain directions as I meander through life. The first guideline is obvious in keeping with the premise of the whole book: *love yourself and practise loving yourself.* It is the keystone to my whole approach to living a happy life and it is the 'secret of life' if there ever was one. The second guideline requires a little more introduction.

When I talk about loving myself, I sometimes have to remind myself that such a statement can be very hard to explain, as how you love yourself is something entirely personal. It can be very difficult for some of us to consciously work at because there are so many variables in our lives and love has of course been infamously difficult to quantify. The first guideline therefore needs something to help make sense of it!

I see the second guideline as a statement of fact. It states that: *we are where we are in life as a direct result of the choices we have made, including choosing not to make a decision, and every choice we make is intended to be the best choice for us personally, based upon the belief system, values, experience and knowledge we possess.* NB: some people's belief systems might serve to dispute this guideline, claiming that karma, God or destiny can impact upon where we find ourselves, but I once again ask you all to suspend your existing beliefs for a short time, if only to look at the alternative

The second guideline is a statement of logic which grows in significance the more we think about it. It takes time to break it down, to take each small group of words and understand what they are saying. It takes time to apply it to the individual parts of your life and allow yourself to feel the repercussions of what it is saying and it takes even more time to reassemble everything back into a working guideline. It is almost like being given the 'code' to read a secret map filled with symbols. It allows you to slowly make sense of the map. It allows you to challenge your initial understanding of the symbols, enabling you to decipher its hidden meaning. Gradually, your code will allow the map to grow in clarity until you can fully understand it and all other maps like it. Once you understand the map, you can decide the direction in which you want to travel.

If you apply this guideline to any area of your life, it

has the potential to decode many previously misinterpreted outlooks. It is like the wild card in a game of cards or the master key in a palace of wonders, something you can use almost anywhere. This guideline promotes forgiveness and understanding, pro-activity and motivation. It is the guideline for an approach to life which allows you the freedom to make mistakes and learn from them. It allows us the freedom to love ourselves.

When we try to love ourselves, we often come up with reasons why we might not be deserving of this love. Maybe we told lies or stole something; perhaps we manipulated events or caused the characters of others to be wrongly examined. When we then look at the reasons we have for not loving ourselves, holding a certain outlook on life might validate this lack of love of ourselves. If however we understand that *we are where we are in life as a direct result of the choices we have made, including choosing not to make a decision, and every choice we make is aimed to be the best choice for us personally, based upon the belief system, values, experience and knowledge we possess*, then it is clear that our errors are merely the result of something we once learned that was not necessarily correct. We told lies or stole because we had somehow learned that the outcome our actions produced were the best for us specifically, at that exact moment in time. We perhaps didn't understand the possible severity of these actions and the connotations, or more likely we just hadn't learnt to value ourselves. If our bigger mistakes are merely the result of earlier smaller mistakes then surely the small mistakes that led to the big ones are forgivable and we are, after all, deserving of our own love.

We intrinsically make decisions aimed at getting the result we subconsciously believe will serve us best and what we believe is best for us is learned through our interaction with our environment from when we were only months old. If we learned things that were wrong because our guardians didn't understand what their parenting skills taught us, or indeed that our guardians didn't realise what we were learning despite of what we were being taught, we then developed slightly incorrect beliefs. Our early incorrect beliefs become the building blocks for our whole lives as we try to make the values and actions of those around us make sense.

When we realise that our biggest mistakes are usually the result of many little errors in our learning, small mistakes built upon smaller mistakes, then it makes understanding our mistakes easier, and ultimately more forgivable. Every mistake we make can have repercussions, some more noteworthy than others, some even creating the need for some form of punishment, but ultimately we can find a place in almost all mistakes from where we can start to forgive ourselves.

We can find it easier to forgive ourselves for any perceived transgressions we might have been party to when we understand what has caused them. For example, I can remember cheating in an exam when I was about eighteen and this event became part of my perceived makeup for the next decade of my life. This view I had of myself had underlying repercussions for me and I often gave myself a hard time for my actions. It wasn't until more than a decade later that I was actually free to forgive myself.

When I decided to cheat I knew it was wrong on many levels but I subconsciously decided not to analyse it too much. I had a value conflict between the consequences of doing something that was wrong and the consequences of failing an exam, but I allowed myself to hide from certain truths. My specific circumstances had taught me that academic success was something that I was judged upon and I was motivated by the desire to be judged positively. I had allowed myself to be distracted throughout the duration of this specific course, and my knowledge was not sufficient to gain me a high mark. I was strongly convinced that I wouldn't get caught and I needed to achieve a high mark. I had a choice to make and I chose to cheat.

The reason I had let myself become distracted from my studies were two fold. Firstly, I didn't really like the course. I had embarked on it because I thought it was what certain figures in my life wanted me to do, thus bringing me closer to them. Secondly, due to the fact that academia had previously come quite easily to me, I hadn't really developed my academic 'hard work' ethic.

All through my early childhood I was a relatively high achiever academically. I grew up in a rural area and went to a small school. I enjoyed learning and this was encouraged. When I moved to secondary school two scenarios developed over the first year. Firstly, I believed that my efforts to perform in school had become expected as opposed to appreciated. I was now amongst a larger number of similarly academic peers, and whilst at first I excelled, subconsciously I felt my achievements weren't being rewarded or appreciated enough to warrant the effort put in. On top of this, school excellence, or more so, scholastic superiority, was never going to win me a popularity contest amongst my peers.

Like a lot of us in our early teens, I identified more with my peers than with my family and this led me to hold time spent with my peers in higher regard. As I moved through school, I slowly managed to study less and less. I held the belief that the pain of diligent study needed to produce an outcome of feeling special through rewards or success. This outcome would have to overshadow the anguish of being seen as a 'swot', the loss of free time and the possibility of failure. If it didn't seem likely that study would be rewarded, then there was no point in making an effort. It was simple logic.

A lot can be explained if we look at our values in relation to our identity. As a teen, the value of being valued was one of my key motivators. This was pertinent as one of my most significant personal opinions, because I almost always felt like I was the odd one out in any environment I found myself. It makes sense to suggest that someone who holds this type of perspective in relation to the values stated, might be motivated to behave in a way that avoids giving their peers a reason to dislike them.

My family? As I mentioned earlier, I love them all dearly, but at that time I had issues with all of them. I could point out problems with each of them, leaving them all at fault for my deficiencies. I believed that deep down I was always going to be a disappointment to them all. It never actually came into my head that my lack of appreciation for them might encourage them to leave me behind but often, even though my childhood years were generally happy, I was more motivated to impress my friends than to engage my family.

I only felt good about myself when I thought others looked up to me and, again, this was learned from other events throughout my early years. This was not something I was taught, rather it was something I had learned. It created an inner conflict from an early age. This conflict didn't come to the fore when I was at primary school because I was the alpha male in a tiny school in a rural community. Going to secondary school changed my environment and certain things that I had learned no longer applied, I was vulnerable. From a psychological perspective, I adapted, but I did so from a compromised position.

If we move on to my late teens, I was like most people, mixed up. I was a good kid at heart, but I was weighed down by an overwhelming sense of inadequacy. I surrounded myself with friends who individually were better at music, better at sport, funnier, better with girls, better at posturing, and I basically compared myself unfavourably to them all. I was constantly trying to achieve the feeling that others valued me, but I tried to do it in a way that wouldn't bring too much attention, as humility is never far away from a teenager.

The thing with low self esteem is that it is learned. Quite often, you learn it through your interpretation of events rather than it being foisted upon you, although this too can occur. When you have low self esteem you don't value yourself and you find it hard to believe that people can value you either. People with low self esteem either struggle with sadness throughout their lives or try to reinvent themselves in the hope that they can fake it a bit until they find happiness through being appreciated by others. Most that do this enter a debilitating circle.

And yet most of the pain and misunderstanding is avoidable. If it is learned, which I truly believe it is in 99.9% of cases, then it can be unlearned. What is more, if it is learned through people developing incorrect opinions, then we can simply apply a little more awareness into our lives and prevent ourselves from being party to the same issues with our own kids.

I had come to believe that my value as a person was based solely upon the opinion of others and I learned this through a series of tiny events, communications and assumptions. This theory was based upon the incorrect belief that I was my parent's least favourite child and I needed to constantly impress them or I would become unloved. This was never the case, but it became a central belief for over twenty years of my life. If I had only learned that this was just because my parents showed affection in a different way than other families and that I was indeed loved unconditionally, then I would never have associated my value with *being good at stuff*.

As parents, how we communicate or show love stems from our experiences of our own upbringing. If my parents had understood the complexities of how I saw the world, they would have instantly done everything in their power to show me how loved I actually was. My parents did everything they could to give me and my siblings everything they thought would serve us best in the world.

Today, as I pass through certain stages of my life, aware of
how I react in a world of readily available information and
opinion, I look at my approach to parenting and I
understand their's so much better.

Through a series of beliefs, some of which were wrong,
I developed belief systems. As I grew, I interpreted the
world in relation to my beliefs and inevitably I made
miscalculations: we all do. Due to my ever evolving
opinion of my world and my specific position within it,
through no fault of anyone, I developed a self esteem
problem which impacted the next twenty years of my life.

I spent my late teens and most of my twenties asking
myself: "Would I go back in time and change my past if I
could? Would I go back in time and change certain things I
had done? Would I go back and tell my parents that I just
wanted to be told I was loved no matter what?" I spent
almost ten years arriving at a different variation of the same
answer: "Absolutely". I spent ten years drifting in and out of
a daydream, wondering what my life could have been if
only I had done things differently. I spent a decade either
standing on the sidelines of life, afraid to get fully involved,
or reinventing myself in the hope that I could find happiness.

In my past, every time I tried to love myself, I would
stumble upon a reason why I felt undeserving of true love.
This would always be reason enough to stop looking too

deep. When I eventually resolved to make a concerted effort to truly love myself I was able to revisit these reasons and slowly my results changed. I was able to attribute these undeserving feelings to either something I did, something someone else did or my perception of the actions of others. If the reason I was undeserving of my own love was due to something I had done then I was gradually able to forgive myself, because whatever I had done was due to me trying to take the best course of action for me.

This 'course of action' was relative to my understanding of the circumstances (learned), my understanding of the environment (learned) my understanding of my abilities (learned), my values (learned) and the consequences of my actions (learned). Quite simply, any deficiency I might have had was learned and theoretically it was merely a culmination or small forgivable mistakes. These mistakes may have called for some form of punishment, but everything was ultimately worthy of forgiveness.

Soon, I was able to look at the actions of others in the same way as I looked at my own. Some of the actions of others merited consequence, but regardless of this, these were simply actions that they had learned were acceptable. I began to realise that my interpretations of the actions of others was often more about my perceptions of their actions and my ability to react confidently to them, than the actions themselves. I began to look at the mistakes of others in the same way as I looked at my own mistakes without having to understand them. Big mistakes were generally the culmination of smaller mistakes, all flaws in learning, all eventually forgivable. As they say in the world of computers: garbage in, garbage out!

The combination of loving yourself and forgiving yourself is like melting a glacier. It is a very gradual event and you are unsure of what you will uncover. On the face of it, it can appear that nothing is changing, however you feel the difference. The more you love yourself the more love you have within you. The more love you have within you, the easier and more natural it becomes to feel love and naturally you become more forgiving. The more you forgive the more loving you feel outwardly and with this, more of the world's negativities ebb away. All the time that the glacier is melting, it is losing mass. The pressures which it previously placed on that which lies underneath lessen, and what lies underneath starts to change. The change of pressure results in a shifting of the ground (you) which lies underneath. The reductions of these pressures might initially show itself in momentous movements or reactions, however after a period of time and re-positioning, everything is allowed to return to its natural form, allowed to be itself, the best itself it can be, whatever the environment.

We live in a society that has somehow overlooked the basest lesson of all, which is to love yourself first. As a result of this, rules have been created, evolving throughout the history of mankind, which have left it inevitable that we will have rule and value conflicts. Although we are where we are as a society and as individuals directly due to the decisions of our ancestors, we cannot blame them as the basis for their decision making was flawed. If all decisions were based upon a flawed philosophy, then the mistakes of the past are forgivable.

If we look at ourselves and where we stand in life, understanding that all the things we blame ourselves and others for have simply been the result of the culmination of mistakes, it is easier to accept where we are and forgive those whom have impacted on us. This forgiveness, accepting and non-judgemental entity, when we appreciate it and take ownership of it, is love.

LOVE AND GOD

"Love is always patient and kind; it is never jealous; love is never boastful or conceited; it is never rude or selfish; it does not take offence, and it is not resentful. Love takes no pleasure in other people's sins but delights in the truth; it is always ready to excuse, to trust, to hope and to endure whatever comes."

A letter from Paul to the Corinthians (13:04).

Throughout the ages, love has been a notoriously evasive subject when anyone has tried to put it into words. Most of us can recognise what it feels like but struggle to explain what it actually is. For me, the words above, words that were recorded almost two thousand years ago, capture my perception of love wonderfully.

It portrays love as a very simple philosophy. It doesn't try to contain what love might be through some form of qualification, nor does it define itself to a chosen few through a man-made limitation. It seems like a very attainable, very real possibility but significantly it also reads as if it were describing the traits of a person. As I have said before, a religious view of God is not something that I believe in, yet in my past this had left me partially restricted. I had previously resigned myself to the belief that God could not exist, as God must only exist in the way I had been directed to understand him by those who seemed to be most involved with him/her/it.

When we think about the words of St Paul, it does not take too much imagination to replace 'love' with 'God'. God is always patient and kind; he is never jealous; *God is never boastful or conceited; he is never rude or selfish; he does not take offence, and he is not resentful. God takes no pleasure in other people's sins but delights in the truth; he is always ready to excuse, to trust, to hope and to endure whatever comes.* A very simple representation of a Christian God? It seems strange that two such concepts are merely words apart. Is it possible that ancient explanations of love and its omnipotent humility could somehow have strengthened the definitions of today's Christian God?

It is not for me to dictate how others view love, religion or their God because everyone sees the world from their own perspective. However, in order to explain myself I must try to clarify the terms I use. When I am required to think of, or read about, God from a modern or religious perspective, it is almost certain that people are speaking about the bearded, forgiving man who resides in heaven, an entity I don't believe in. In the past this created a conflict within me. I didn't believe in him and this left me at best excluded from a primarily religious society.

When I originally decided that the existence of God was not possible, it was because I was shunning the man-made God created by religion or more specifically, the Catholic Church. Initially I went through the 'I don't believe in that, so everyone must be wrong' phase. It was only natural to believe that those bound by a religious God were always going to be stuck in a restrictive cycle. I could see people whose lives would always be limited because they had faced challenges beyond those which their God was made for. I saw people waiting for intervention and people who felt they were beyond redemption. There were people who believed that an omnipotent God would judge them at their weakest and people who thought all they had to do to be good was to look good in the eyes of the church.

In those days I didn't have an answer and it left me on the outside. I remember talking to a wise older gentleman and during one specific conversation about nothing in particular he turned to me and said, "It was easy to have faith when I was young, I wouldn't like to know what you now know." I felt at odds with the conspiracy theory that excluded me!

Ten years ago when I still believed in this man-made God, when I could actually still argue the point for 'his' existence, I felt somewhat uneasy with the conflicting images of a Christian God. What was he like? Was he wise and forgiving or was he vengeful and full of wrath? On good days he was like the best friend I could ever imagine but on the not so good days he would evaluate my every move, waiting to catch me out. Ultimately this God, with his split personality, created thousands of years ago, was always going to be something more magnificent than I could ever understand, and eventually he would judge me in a way that I was too unholy to comprehend.

Throughout my life I had this overwhelming belief in the distinct possibility that some magical Godly (or unGodly) force was one day possibly going to solve all my woes. I hoped it would forgive me for the mistakes I made because it understood the challenges I failed, yet at the same time I felt there was the possibility that I might have already taken the step too far into eternal damnation. I believed in hope more than anything, that there was the tiniest of possibilities that a just God could forgive my sins and accept that any wrongs I committed were not because of any evil that existed within me, but rather they were the result of my weakness or naivety. All the while I feared that as a result of what I had read, learned and observed that if we made in likeness of God, then he was too judgmental to let me off!

These are thoughts similar to those which many of us

might have had, and many a well versed person could use them to suggest whatever they wanted you to believe: that God is vengeful or that he is all forgiving. It was this 'matter of opinion' which made me take a step back in relation to my belief in God. There was evil all over the world; espionage and deceit, murder and theft, rape and molestation, poverty and greed, and God was residing over it all. Religions and faiths, kings and government found it easy to claim they were following God's will when it suited them. Indeed, God was often used as justification for many an atrocity. But no, this was not God. These things were happening because God was merely a man-made God, used by the powerful to remain in power.

It took me a significant amount of time to fully commit myself to feeling that there was no possible way that the God I grew up believing in could exist, and when it happened I felt empty. I immediately started my search to replace him. As mentioned earlier, I chased many paths and beliefs to try to find an answer for which I had no real question. I wanted to feel that there was some semblance of sense to my existence that allowed me to be free from the nonsense and superstition, yet still allowed me to dream of the wonders of what might be.

With all this said and done I examined possibility after possibility, before asking myself this;

"What if there was no God. What would happen?

Would the world descend into anarchy? Is there a force which exists that transcends religion and race, colour and creed that might help us know what to do? What force might exist, that is truly able to understand what within me is forgivable and what repentance I needed to offer for my wrong doings? If the only known force is love, and love makes you feel happy, and to feel unconditional love gives you the strength to do the right thing simply because it is the right thing, might loving yourself be the key to everything?"

It was astounding. In that instant I no longer thought about God in any biblical sense. The entity I was seeking already existed and it was called *Love*. Love needed no form, nor was it defined in terms of physicality or personality. No-one could claim the exclusive rights over it and no one was truly excluded from it by another. Within weeks of this transition of thought, of going from not believing a God could exist to not caring if one did or not, instead embracing love as the answer to everything, I simply observed that love was the key to everything.

CLEARING THE SLATE

It is not for me to tell you how to see the world nor is it for me to set rules for how you should live your life. That is not how it works. I would hope that you see enough in my theory, regardless of how you view the world, to appreciate that we are all more capable of living life happily when we feel love for ourselves and use our own rules. If we love ourselves unconditionally we will create a state of love within us from which we will do the right thing. When we act from a place of love we can very effectively live a happy and healthy life and will not need to be told what to do.

If we are happy, then we will perceive the world from a happier perspective and if we love ourselves and forgive ourselves we will feel happier more often. This becomes a positive cycle of loving and forgiving which combines to increase the incidence of happiness. Loving ourselves automatically leads to forgiving ourselves and forgiving ourselves leaves room to love ourselves a little more. Collectively, you can't help but feel happier when you love and forgive yourself.

I can remember when I first started to 'practise loving and forgiving myself', I had a lot of issues to face. They were my issues and although they might seem small to certain people, they were very real and, what is more, each one was wrapped up in another, like a tangle of knots. It slowly became obvious to me that a lot of what had affected me could be traced back to simple mistakes from my childhood and these mistakes were likely to have had weightier consequences than perhaps they merited. I needed to start again from scratch; I needed to clear the slate.

When I first started to trace the issues that I had back to their origins, I found a whole barrage of emotions started to rush towards me, and quite often they would knock me sideways. I hadn't expected this. I expected the process of loving myself to be the equivalent of slipping into an emotional hot tub, being soothed and refreshed as all my woes left me, but instead I found myself being hit from all angles by something which resembled cold water from a power hose.

In trying to love myself, I found other emotions creep up on me. These emotions which had been kept under the surface often appeared with an accompanying feeling of vulnerability. Soon, mixed emotions in their rawest forms became muddled up and presented themselves as a feeling of anger: anger with myself, with people and the world. I didn't necessarily have to have a specific reason for feeling angry; it just seemed to be the result of a build up of pressures that had culminated over the years. I'm not sure how this might be for others, but for me it was a very uncertain and unsettling time.

When you start to face those things that you have tucked away inside of you, you have to stand face to face with a whole range of facades. You will view parts of yourself that you might previously have avoided. You might observe characteristics that you've learned to improve upon and you might even look at elements of yourself that you have learned to severely dislike. This can be the hardest part. This first step is often so big that it seems too difficult because we fear what might be around the corner.

No matter what you face, there are two things to keep in mind at this time. Firstly, this is a process of forgiving, and everything can be forgiven if you wish it to be, even if you have to spend twenty years in jail to atone for a particular mistake. Secondly, almost everyone has a secret that they don't want their friends or family to know about, because they believe people will think less of them.

Once you begin to understand why you did or thought what you did, that led to the mistake or the development of a trait, you can start to forgive yourself. This 'getting to know yourself' is a gradual process which can be slow, but it is an honest process. It uncovers your mistakes and lets you take ownership of them. It will allow you to understand these mistakes and their consequences, and the motivations which led to them. It isn't about blaming or transferring guilt. It is about taking responsibility for our own actions through understanding them, understanding the consequences we might not previously have been aware of and empowering ourselves one step at a time.

When you get into the habit of loving and forgiving yourself and those around you, it can be quite shocking how much certain things change with regard to your outlook. As you begin to accept the mistakes you have made and forgive yourself, slowly cultivating more love within, you begin to look at the world around you in a whole new way, you start to get stronger.

After some time spent to-ing and fro-ing, trying to understand my new world, I had managed to clear enough space in my own head to stop judging myself. I had decided to accept who I was and how I got here. I resolved to stop trying to reinvent myself. My belief at the time was that this would allow me to decide in which direction I wanted to go.

Previous attempts at doing something similar to 'drawing a line under things' had failed. I had, in my time, bought into more than one self-help strategy but now I realised that I had to go beyond the rules and strategies that were previously offered to me. Nearly every philosophy included the belief that;

- There is a force that I may or may not be able to comprehend which is of another spiritual level to humans.
- I will be required to take a leap of faith in order to connect with this force.
- There will be people who can make sense of the will of this force better than me and they will pass down rules.
- It is only by following this set of rules that I will achieve a true happiness.
- If the rules are changed by those in a position to do so, I must accept that it has either been instructed by God or the strategic leader, for the good of us all.
- Failure to follow these rules will lead to at worse damnation, at best unhappiness.
- The people who created the rules will find themselves in positions of influence and power over those who follow the rules.
- This society needs money to survive, your money.

Every time I had previously committed myself to a strategy, I had failed. I never found the happiness I needed. It was trial and error that dictated that clearing the slate meant I had to go back to a point before someone told me how to be happy.

In trying to understand a philosophy, religion or self help strategy, we must follow a set of rules set down by an individual or group whose perspective on life is guaranteed to be different than ours. How did the instigator of said theory come up with their rules? They applied their previous rules until they didn't work and then created new rules that did work. They then decided that as this was successful for them it could be successful for others. It was up to them to develop a strategy or create a story for teaching these new rules, again based upon their own life experiences, and it is up to the follower or reader to find a way to apply them. This continually perpetuating outlook will always come up short as life is, quite simply, relative.

So, what then am I suggesting? I suggest that the only rules which will, en masse, work for you, are rules that can fully sit alongside your understanding of the world. In either creating your own rules or accepting the rule set of others, you must accept that others will have their own rules too. No two sets of rules will be identical as we all have personal experiences which dictate our actions and reactions. In order for you to create your own rule base, you must first reach an understanding of your world and decide where you want to fit in. When we look at the society we live in, it is fair to say that a majority of the laws and moral guidelines we have, serve their purpose well. In fact, if I look at my own particular society, and cross reference it with any of the great faiths or philosophies, we can see an almost seamless equilibrium at the top end. Don't kill, don't steal, show love and forgive, give thanks and help others; all 'rules' worth adhering to in my opinion.

Throughout history, there have been people who examined the rules which existed and decided that they were flawed. Continually, the greatest thinkers of our civilisation have looked at the theories which sat alongside faiths and provided new elucidations from them. Leaps of faith and interpretations have created Gods from men, created miracles from natural events and led our ancestors to believe that the sun revolved around the earth. The removal of these misinformed interpretations which have previously been used to explain events and 'prove' theories, creates the need for us to look closer at what remains.

Look at your own general family storyline history or even your own personal history. How much of that which you believed ten years ago do you believe now? How much of what your parents believed when they where eighteen do they now conform to? I would guess that there are very different answers out there as each answer is, again, from a personal perspective. A majority of people mould their key values slowly unless some large external force creates a conflict, whilst their day to day values are quite malleable, depending usually on environment, mood and context. If you have siblings, then it is fair to say that how you were treated in relation to them depends upon how your parents own experiences shaped their views of the world. You were probably raised slightly different to your siblings, as your parents or guardians had differing impressions of each of your personalities. They would hold different views on how to deal with you in relation to different circumstances, as well as a contextual outlook of each impacting event, based upon how they saw the world at that precise point.

As we grow, so too do the layers of our subconscious outlook. We learn what we learn in relation to many factors related to the lesson. For example, who is teaching us, how are they teaching us? What is their mood? What are they trying to teach? What do I previously know about the subject? What motivates me to learn? All these things and many more shape small lessons, with each small lesson learned coming together to create our subconscious overview. If we have subconsciously taken rules and outlooks onboard because they were seen as unquestionable truth in the past, then it is possible that we could adjust our outlook and start afresh.

Clearing the slate is not about starting from zero, removing all that we believe in and stampeding aimlessly towards anarchy. It is not about collapsing in a corner tearfully wondering why you are where you are. It is about accepting that the world is, very simply, where it has chosen to be. You are, where you have chosen to be, based on the fact that you have made decisions (or not as the case may be) to get here. The collective decisions or avoidance of decisions, were made based upon where you were at said time.

Clearing the slate, is about accepting that, whether you feel happy or sad, lost or found, you have within you all the tools you need to be happy. There are people who are reading this who are just looking for a little change of perspective, and there are some people who have been drawn to read this as they feel they are already at a point of desperation. It doesn't matter where you are. Clearing the slate will help you start to remove the labels that have been forced upon you, and allow you to find a true happiness in just being you.

Clearing the slate is about saying "let's stop judging others by our rules and stop judging ourselves by theirs." It is about looking at the possibility of learning to love ourselves unconditionally and moving on. It is about feeling alive to where you are at this moment, realising how you arrived here and **feeling** what you know you should do. It's about starting again with the basic belief that you can love yourself unconditionally in order to make sense of your world, and ultimately be happy and trust yourself enough to know you'll find your own way.

It might not seem easy for some, and it may look impossible for others, but the only thing that will stop you loving yourself is the opinion that you don't deserve to do so. This perception has been created by your conditioning and it is wholly wrong. Stop judging yourself, clear the slate and give loving yourself a chance.

YOU CHOOSE

So there we are, the first part of the book is over and it is time for you to make a choice. You have read what I have to say and you must decide for yourself what you want to do with it. Do you agree with my theory of loving yourself or do you not? Do you test drive the theory a little more or do you fully commit to loving yourself? Maybe you decide not to make any decisions just yet! No matter what you decide to do, you should make a decision so that you are at the very least going in a direction that you choose. This way if you ever need to look back, to identify a point of choice and work out why perhaps you are not where you hoped to be, you can.

Throughout the previous chapters, I have strived to show the difference between my theories on understanding and achieving happiness and things that I believe limit our understanding of happiness, like organised religions, Gods and 'secret of life' schemes. I make this distinction because it is important. I see the world my way and have my own experiences, and this has led me to arrive at a view of the world which says that if I learn to love myself unconditionally, I will gradually be more loving and forgiving and thus happier. This basic theory does not require you to see the world how I see it, nor does it ask you to forsake your beliefs. Everyone has their own way of seeing things.

I am motivated by fact that there are a lot of unhappy people in the world who are led to convoluted, exclusionary, man-made, self-important theories in their search for happiness, often spending significant amounts of money, time or energy on something which cannot be collectively found out with them. Concepts and strategies are sold, offering systems or rules you must adhere to, or rules you must follow in order to achieve happiness, and this is wrong. There is no singular external fix. Those who create and sell these systems ultimately know that, as they cannot factor individual aspects of your life into their system, it will not be the catch-all solution it claims to be. They accept there are flaws, but they will paper over it and sometimes even suggest that your inability to carry out their 'conditions' is the reason for the identification of any flaw.

I have suggested that the key is removal of the misconceptions created throughout history, misconceptions which have been brought about as a reaction to a challenge of a weakness in a story. The constant re-ordering of what is allowed or not, in any given philosophy or group, aimed at covering up the failings in any given philosophy which only become noticeable after time, is simply moving the goalposts in order to survive. These goalposts will be continually moved until someone points out how far they have been moved, by whom and for what reason. This person or persons may then stand up and suggest that the new position is simply too far removed from the supposed cast iron original location. I suggest the removal of rules applied by others to our lives under the premise of governance, to make way for simple theory, that happiness is relative and loving yourself is the key to true happiness.

I suggest the things above so that you might give yourself a guilt free, condition free opportunity to try the simplest of things without fear of doing it wrong. The process of understanding and the actuating of 'loving yourself' is a personal journey, and it is about a way of thinking rather than a quick fix. Only you truly know how you view yourself in relation to the world and even that perception changes. So, being the only constant in your life, you are the only place to start. Loving yourself and forgiving yourself go hand in hand, and the better understanding we have of how we came to where we are, the easier it is to separate what is fact from what is perceived and decide how we want to progress.

What are your thoughts? Would you agree with what

I am suggesting? Where do you want to go from here? Is it worth a try? Well, before you decide on whether you would like to embrace 'loving yourself' I would ask you to read one last thing. Any theory is workable as long as it stays within the confines of normality. What happens when we are talking about extremes or possibly just very real emotional events?

The theory behind *Find Me Happy* is about two main things. It is about clearing off the shackles and limitations you had previously developed, through a process of loving and forgiving yourself, in order to be truly happy and it is about moving forward from a point of forgiveness through loving yourself habitually. When we embark on a journey of loving and forgiving ourselves, we become aware of our core values and we start to re-examine them to decide if anything needs updating. We start to make sense of our own life, deciding what we want to keep and what we want to leave behind.

What are our values? How did they come about? Do we still hold the same beliefs which led to us embracing them in the first place? We tend to have a few values we aspire to, lofty values that we would love to live by yet sometimes fall short of; values shown to us by our parents or our communities, designed to direct us towards what is perceived to be the best way to live our lives. These values sit side by side the everyday, less demanding values which we live by. It is, after all, hard to be perfect. Maybe another way of looking at this is that we strive to have values that society appreciates and we live to the values that allow us to make our best way through our day to day lives. It is similar to living a few of our own rules and aspiring to live by some of the rules of others. We might know why we should do something, like eat less or exercise more, but the true way we see both ourselves and the world complicates things.

When you start to love and forgive yourself, you start to re-establish your true values. These are values that only exist because you believe them to be right and you automatically (re) engage with them to take true ownership of them. They range from base values you live every day, to values you might work towards once a year, and they could show themselves through not flying with a certain airline or not eating a certain product, to making the conscious effort to be charitable in your interactions. You might work at developing certain traits or simply you might put more effort into everything. As you grow to love yourself, the ownership of your values will grow also. Loving yourself affords you the freedom to develop the courage of your convictions, and it also allows you the time to work out what these convictions might be.

As you continue to love and forgive yourself, your method of interaction with the world slowly changes. That which you believe in becomes something you now have the courage to protect without fear, because loving yourself allows you the clarity to embrace your own ideals without worrying about what others might think. You don't try to change people, because you understand that everyone sees things their own way as a result of their own experiences and beliefs. You don't have an ego to protect, as you realise that an ego comes merely through the fear of what others think. You can live your life without the stress of worrying "what should I do?"

Loving yourself first is about being free and about being true, but sometimes in life that might actually leave you in conflict with other sets of rules, for example: laws. How you resolve any situation that offers this conflict is entirely up to you but suffice to say, any decision you make will be from a strong perspective, and any repercussions of said decision are acceptable, even if you make the wrong choice.

This is the road that loving yourself will put you on. You might look at yourself and decide you have done things which you have not yet redressed honestly, or you might feel the need to change your direction, if where you were going is no longer the place you want to go.

I believe some people find these possibilities overwhelming and even scary due to their lack of self belief. If that applies to you, do not worry. Self belief is learned, so the lack of it means that you probably haven't had the opportunity to show yourself your true depth of character. Today might not be the day that you commit to loving yourself. If today you feel that this direction isn't for you, then you should neither give yourself or this theory a hard time. Just accept your feelings and make a decision on what to do next. If you think however that loving yourself first is the thing for you, then let's start!

LEARNING TO LOVE YOURSELF

Find yourself a quiet space, somewhere you can relax and allow yourself the time and privacy to do a short exercise in imagination. You might want to read the next three paragraphs through in order to know fully what you are trying to imagine, but try not to read any further for the time being as it might affect your train of thought.

First things first, breathe. Most of us have either forgotten or have never really learned the true potential of breathing. Try it now! Sit in a relaxed but upright position and breathe in and out, deeply, ten times. For each breath in and out, count slowly to seven and try to maintain a similar intensity with each individual breath. As you come towards the end of each breath, make sure you fill or empty your lungs respectively. In its basest of forms, breathing is simply the process of removing toxins from our blood cells and replacing the toxins with the oxygen we need. As with all muscles, if we don't exercise the muscles that work our lungs to their fullest capacity, gradually we will lessen the efficiency of our breathing. Our body feels stressed when our oxygen levels drop, so often when something happens that might deplete our oxygen stores we find deep breathing helps. Instead of waiting for the 'stress', we should aim to keep our oxygen stores full and fresh. The following exercise works best if we incorporate a breathing exercise like mentioned above.

Imagine you were in a state of complete love. Being in a state of love is not the same as being in love with someone or having someone love you, rather it is simply you feeling love. This exercise can be hard to get your head around as I am asking you to take something which is difficult to describe and use it in a way that you have probably never tried before. If you find this a step too far, we'll take a step back. Try to remember that pure feeling of love you had for a newborn, or the pure feeling you felt for your first love. Perhaps you can remember the feeling of safety in the arms of a loved one, or the feeling you had when someone loved you, or maybe you can remember the grateful feeling you had when someone you loved did something special for you. Try to take one or more of these feelings and remove any exterior conditions from them and just concentrate on the love. Imagine the feeling of unconditional love building up within you, there simply because you can and you are able to have it within you.

Take your time to explore what this feels like as the feeling changes from nothing, to something that fills you up. It can start in your toes or in your fingers, your head, your heart or your belly. Remember, there are no rules to this, it is just about how you feel. Try to imagine what it might look like. Does it resemble a swirling, brightly coloured sphere inside you, growing in size and intensity? Does it tingle? Maybe it is like a body of water filling you up. Maybe it has a sound or a smell; maybe it makes you feel weightless. This exercise will probably be a new experience so I would suggest that you do it at your own speed for as long and as often as you want. As with anything, practise improves application.

Like any new skill, some of you will find it easier and some of you might struggle a little. Some people will have experience of similar relaxation exercises, and some of you might never have been asked to do anything like this. It is the same as a sport. Some people are more natural and others have transferable skills. Some find the skills hard to develop and some of us feel too vulnerable to even want to try.

Skills benefit from proper practise. The most skilful athlete needs to practise even though their skill is more acute than the rest of us might ever understand, and those who become complacent in their ability tend to lose their edge! Practise the ability to build up love inside you by using your own experiences of love and then removing any and all conditions or attachments. Like practising the ability to first catch a ball straight in front of you and then honing that skill to be able to anticipate a ball coming from any direction, if you practise working with love you will be ready to recognise it and accept it more easily. When you have tried this quite a few times and you feel you are able to build up a sufficient amount of love inside you, holding it for perhaps fifteen minutes, comfortable that distraction will not cause the feeling to run away, you are ready to apply your new skill.

Now, imagine what it might be like to be in two places at once with one version of yourself lying relaxed on your bed and the other version standing lovingly, watching over you. This might seem a bit difficult at first so if you feel the need, you can start by lying down and imagining that someone nice and loving is standing over you like a guardian. Once you have visualised this for a short time, stand up to swap places with the other person imagining them lying down. When you are relaxed enough to hold this visualisation, it is time to begin the next little exercise.

Try to build the feeling of love you were previously practicing and see if you can hold it for three minutes. When you are comfortable maintaining the feeling of love within you, try to picture yourself in the position of the person standing over yourself. As the person standing, hold the love within you for a little longer and then gradually attempt to move that love from you to the person on the bed. Let it pour in such a way that the love you have within you, the giver, is unending and the love that you are giving is received instantaneously. Try to sustain this feeling of love you have built up and the feeling of giving love to another for five minutes.

When you are comfortable with this, it is time to take the next step. Try to slip out of the body of the giver and into the body of the receiver. Imagine what it is like to receive a river of unconditional love from another person. Let that love wash over and through you and feel it penetrate every part of your body, mind and soul.

If this is getting difficult, you should try to push on a little bit more before stopping and appreciating what you have done. This might be very new to you, so take it slowly. What we are trying here is simply a technique in learning to love yourself. The most important thing is that you find a way to love yourself so it is possible that a different method may suit you better. With that said, this technique is worth experimenting with a bit over a month or two before you contemplate discarding it in search of another.

You should try and build up the sensation of giving love, and take particular heart in the fact that the love is coming from an unending supply and going to another unconditionally. It is not for you to judge who is worthy of receiving. You are simply giving away love and letting the receiver deal with receiving. If you can't manage ten minutes on your first go I would ask that you attempt this exercise twice more before you read another word!

LOVE YOURSELF PART B

Hopefully you will have given yourself a chance to do the exercise efficiently as laid out in the last chapter. This is really about doing things for your own benefit and not cutting corners. If you cut corners you are more likely to miss some of the benefits of the lesson, so please make sure you are comfortable with feeling love for yourself and receiving love from yourself before reading on!

By this stage you should have built up your ability over a number of attempts, to a point where you are confident at collecting love within you and feeling it grow to a stage where you sense that it is infinite. Hopefully you are comfortable in feeling this love and picturing it in a visualisation as discussed in the last chapter. You should be able to feel yourself loving and, ultimately, loving yourself. After sustaining that, you should then be able to slip into the body of the receiver on the bed and feel comfortable accepting the love that you are offering.

How does it feel to receive real love from yourself? For some, this will seem a simple enough task and for others it can be hard. Regardless of how easy or hard you find it, I suggest you make sure you give yourself a chance to do it properly. Whatever you feel after doing this will show you what you need to do. Take as much time as you need and try to feel the emotions that are showing themselves to you.

What did you feel when you completed the exercise? Did you feel anything? Were you aware of any thoughts? Quite often, when people comment on how they felt after they attempted to love themselves unconditionally, they talk of three things. Firstly, there is the possibility that they didn't really feel anything. This can be for a number of reasons but quite simply put, it is best to keep practising! The second group, the group that we are least likely to fit in, find the process natural and affirming and feel no adverse reactions from the exercise, almost like they had been doing something like it all their life!

The most likely initial outcome of the exercise is that you will have found yourself in the middle ground, struggling to get that feeling of love going or perhaps feeling not quite deserving of the love. This is where a vast majority of us will find ourselves and your feelings will dictate what you should do next. If you are struggling with the process as a whole, then you should try again to break the process down into parts. Don't break your neck to change habits of your lifetime; there is no sense in rushing this. Practise and make an effort and don't let any negative thoughts distract you or make excuses on your behalf. Remind yourself that you are simply trying to love yourself without condition and this is something worth persevering at.

If you lean more towards feeling not truly worthy of the love you offered yourself, you are well on the way to loving yourself. The reason for this is that, due to the societies we live, in it is nearly impossible not to have some negative opinion of ourselves deep within us, gained through an interaction of some sort. It is these pointers that lead us to unravel the unnecessary conflicts or opinions we have created of ourselves.

Another significant question we should be asking is "what is it that suggests to us that we might not be deserving of our own love?" Is it ourselves, our own voice offering a logical reason or justification, or is it our 'inner voice'? If it is our own voice then we can talk to ourselves to accept whatever it is that stops us loving ourselves, allowing us to remove it as a blockage, through forgiveness. If, however, it is the voice of our inner self, the critical voice that sometimes contradicts us or points out our failings, what do we do?

I briefly mentioned this voice at the start of this book, and the term 'inner voice' is widely spoken about. It alludes to a voice that speaks to us when we are not consciously directing it, a voice of another part of us that cannot necessarily be controlled. Various people and groups have tried to explain our inner voice, especially when they are looking to decipher it in response to how it has been portrayed, but I look at it from a simpler stance.

This voice that we have within us is merely the legacy of our childhood. People have given this inner voice a lot of time and thought but in truth this voice is nothing more than a made up character with its roots in childhood role playing. If we observe children playing with toys, they usually talk out loud (although some prefer to imagine it) to best serve their game. Even when a child is unhappy with their parent, sibling or peer, they often feel compelled to role-play the recent events to better deal with what has happened.

Think of our own childhood games and conversations we had, as we played on our own where we were required to invent a character to communicate with. This character, depending upon the situation, could know little, or more pertinently, know everything. We learned to layer the voice through role playing. Through our formative years, the scope of possibilities of the inner voice or character is fine tuned as our mind explores our opinion of ourselves and the world around us. Depending upon our own experiences, outlook and thoughts, the voice will have become what we made it. We should never see it as anything more than an elaborate character we made up.

So if there is a negative voice inside our head that seems to be providing an obstruction to the process of loving ourselves, we can now see this voice for what it is, an automated response conditioned over the years through role playing. It is not a separate entity. It can't really 'tell' us anything, it is simply a character we have developed over the years speaking from the simplistic voice of our childhood.

Recapping, chapter 8 is a formulated attempt to love ourselves, aimed at supporting those who might struggle to love themselves without the aid of a technique. It is a technique I devised to help me love myself to overcome many little blockages, but it is by no means the only way to love yourself. Loving yourself is the key to unravelling the negativities tangled throughout the way you view yourself, allowing you to take a firm forward step in forgiving yourself, loving yourself and understanding your own happiness. By creating a habit of this exercise you will become more fluent in handling love and you will understand that anything that presents itself, to suggest you are not fully worthy of love, is only a signpost to an issue that needs resolving.

As we have already explained, every mistake that we make is the result of making a decision that we thought would serve us best. The miscalculation that led to the mistake is one which will have its origins in a mistake in our learning, a limitation in our capabilities or a conflict of our values, all things which are identifiable and forgivable.

By making a habit of this exercise you will help yourself create and establish a habit of loving yourself, which will slowly increase your general feeling of true happiness and assist in identifying the slight flaws in your armoury that have ultimately affected your self worth. More love means more forgiveness, more forgiveness removes blockages and the removal of blockages leaves more space for love. I would ask that you make a mental note of what you felt when you were giving yourself love or receiving love. These feelings we have, point to how we see our self in relation to giving, judging and receiving. They are signposts, pointing out the direction we must go in order to free ourselves from the limitations we have developed.

If, like me, you felt things were affecting your ability to comfortably complete the process, what did you feel? Was it specific, like, "I am a jealous person so I do not truly deserve love", or was it general and you *felt* undeserving of love? Did you feel uneasy in giving love? Maybe your experiences with giving love have hurt you in the past, or maybe the rules by which you gave love left you vulnerable. Did you feel uneasy in receiving love, perhaps feeling that being loved had conditions? I had already been thinking about loving myself for quite some time before I attempted this, and despite all I knew, I was and still am, very much a work in progress. I have experience in visualising and transferring so that technique was devised as something I knew would work, however I really had very little expectation of what such an experiment might bring.

On one specific occasion when I was getting to grips with building a little love up within me, everything started off well. I was building up love like a swirling, expanding ball of energy and I was experiencing a general feeling of positivity. I imagined the two different versions of myself and stepped into the role of the giver. Within about two minutes, I felt an overwhelming feeling of sadness and I had to stop the whole thing. Although I was in the body of a giver, my subconscious was already two steps ahead and I felt uncomfortable with trying to receive so much love; I had become conscious of trying to give me too much love. In short, no part of me thought I deserved so much love.

I sat stunned and confused. Emotionally I was vulnerable, and physically I felt butterflies in my stomach. I asked myself, "What kind of a person must I be that even in an exercise I struggle to be worthy of love?" I decided to go for a walk and let my head wander to try to make sense of what I was actually feeling.

This mental and physical stroll led me towards a version

of myself in my teenage years, somewhere around the age of fifteen or sixteen. I was visualising myself in the way my subconscious had learned to see me and to my shock, I had a negative picture of the young me in my head. I was seeing a coward of a boy. One who avoided fights and never truly stood up for himself. I can remember knowing that I would have been able to fight back and that I would probably win. I wasn't afraid of being hurt, but I always feared one fight might not be sufficient to end a dispute, and I was afraid of being alone.

As I explored my memory I felt like a fraud because I wasn't as good at school as my parents had hoped. What was worse, I felt like a waste of space because I knew I had it in me to be better at school. I felt guilty for not being a better son or brother. I felt unappealing because I wasn't being chased by girls, and I felt that I was a burden on any team I played for because I wasn't the best athlete. Worst of all, I had stolen a bottle of whiskey from my Granda's cupboard and I felt shallow because I did it to be liked.

As I looked at myself, I started to wonder; "Why was I the way I was? Why was I so afraid to stick up for myself?" There was almost no smacking in our house, and smacking was common in those days, so it wasn't because I had been brought up in an aggressive house and feared violence. In fact, I was brought up very well. There might not have been extra money for luxuries, but I was always safe and secure. We were all well clothed and fed and always well looked after at Christmases and birthdays.

I was smart and could have done better at school, but I didn't have the motivation to do so. I wanted to play and dream and hang out. Part of me wanted to be the smartest person in the world, but as I knew that wasn't possible, I struggled to focus on anything that represented a challenge. I wasn't the best sportsperson either, but in truth I had never been coached in a way that might have helped me learn to enjoy the challenges of sport more. As for stealing from my Grandfather? That was bad. How could I? If I had asked him for the drink he would have probably told me no but explained it was because I was too young. Perhaps he might even have shared a small bottle of beer with me just to show me he understood.

When I tried to love myself I came across a number of reasons why perhaps I wasn't deserving of my own love and it became very clear to me why I had suffered prolonged periods of melancholy throughout my teens and twenties. In its simplest of forms, my opinion of myself was low and it seemed deservedly so. In fact, when I started to think about it, I continually found more and more examples of things that I did which only served to justify my poor opinion of myself. I was just fortunate that I managed to feel a little love for myself before it all threatened to go awry.

I left things for a period of time to let the dust settle on my self appraisal and I moved away from the idea of loving myself. It was bringing me face to face with quite a few demons, and I didn't feel strong enough to look myself in the eye. Luckily, love is like a loyal puppy; it is forgiving and non-judgemental, and seems to understand that sometimes you just need to be nuzzled. That little nuzzle was enough to shake myself from the sadness that my little experience had created and it nudged me a little further towards my two guiding sentences (found in the opening paragraphs of chapter four).

Firstly, I remembered *love yourself and practise loving yourself* and I metaphorically kicked myself on the shin to cut myself a little slack. If I had been observing friends or family members going through the same thing, I would have been ecstatic that they were making an effort to love themselves. I would have been at pains to show them how great they were.

I took a bit of time and thanked myself for having the courage to try loving myself. This self praise did feel a little forced to be honest, but I felt a sense of relief. Once I reminded myself that the term 'practising something' suggests that you can get better at it and that this was one my earliest attempts, I felt a positive resolve that gave me the motivation to keep going, whilst also remembering to go easy on myself.

By the time I ran through my second guideline in my head I felt more at ease with myself. It suggests that *we are where we are in life as a direct result of the choices we have made, including choosing not to make a decision, and every choice we make is aimed to be the best choice for us personally, based upon the belief system, values, experience and knowledge we possess.* It reminded me that every past mistake I made was due simply to not having learned better. I hadn't (in that specific case) learned enough to gain an ability or knowledge, or maybe I had made mistakes in my learning. If I had made or avoided choices because somewhere inside of me this seemed like the best option, then my 'data' or 'tools' must have been wrong! Regardless of the whys and wherefores, my mistakes were not just forgivable but they deserved to be forgiven as they were mistakes I had made when I wasn't ready for the challenge!

I took the knowledge I had and, without being judgemental of myself or anyone involved, I tried to understand where I had come from in order to have made these errors. I also decided to change my approach slightly. I decided that I would take ten minutes every day simply to feel love build up within me to a sufficient amount and then simply let it fill me up. As well as this I decided that I would devote an additional one hour, one day a week, where I would deal with the emotions that had come to the surface and work through them, with the sole purpose of eventually forgiving the mistakes that gave rise to these emotions. I made myself a promise that I would have guaranteed me-time where I could consciously work at forgiving my mistakes and the mistakes of others. And this is what I did.

OTHER STRATEGIES TO GET YOU STARTED

This book is about living life your own way. It is about learning to love yourself as a way to become free from the restrictions which bring about negative perceptions, and it is about finding your own happiness. It is about forgiving ourselves of our past mistakes and moving on to get the best from our future. It is about taking control of our own lives, making decisions and ultimately, being happy.

The act of loving yourself is a personal journey. It can be something we embrace quickly or something that takes time because we struggle to understand some of the key elements. For some, it can help everything else in life make sense, but for others it might initially appear like a step too far. Regardless of how you initially find the act of loving yourself, there is no logical argument in my mind for anything other than loving yourself unconditionally. It is a positive thing, which can only ultimately have positive effects.

It isn't for me to dictate to anyone how they must

access love as, again, that is not what this is about. However, there will be those who require suggestions as to how best to get started. Learning to love ourselves is a personal journey, but we can still support each other to find a way that best suits us. We can observe others and learn from what they achieve, mirroring their success whilst avoiding their mistakes.

If you tried to apply the technique described in the previous chapter and found that you have struggled, there is no cause for concern. There are other techniques that can work alongside loving yourself to support you. Some techniques are mentioned in this chapter and their suitability will depend upon your needs. They are strategies which will make the main technique easier to do and as such they are best used in addition to the main exercise.

Although this whole book works on the premise of you living by your own rules, this does not suggest we throw all existing rules to the side. Instead it asks us to look at the rules we live by and remove the negativities in them through learning to love ourselves and trust our decisions. There are a few undeniable laws of nature that we should not discount and what is more there are coaching techniques that will make them easier to understand and apply. For example, it makes sense that the techniques outlined here will work better with proper practise. The more you practise anything, the easier it will become and any half-hearted attempts serve only to cheapen what you are trying to improve upon. This isn't about someone saying you must do something ten times or one hundred times. It is about understanding that the more efficiently you apply yourself to finding a solution, the higher your possibility of success.

If the technique in the last chapter didn't help you cultivate the feeling of love within yourself, then it is important to find out where the process let you down. If we ask ourselves the following questions, we can pinpoint what needs to be addressed and changed;

- Did you build up love within yourself?
- Did you apply that love to yourself?
- Did you receive the love from yourself?
- Did you choose to give yourself a fighting chance of creating a habit by practising this daily?
- Did you come across an impression of yourself that you struggled to overcome?
- Did you listen to a negative internal opinion of yourself?
- Did you fail in an attempt to forgive yourself for something in the past?

So what was it that distracted us from sticking to the commitment we made to show ourselves the love we deserve? Was it the strategy? Have you applied the strategy without fail for a sufficient amount of time to understand it? If not, ask yourself why you haven't. Are you afraid of something or are you reacting to being told what to do? Are you poor at following instructions or poor at visualising? The answer to these questions will give you an indication of what you should do. Should you perhaps try the technique again, for a longer period of time, with less fear, more humility and a little hope? Or maybe you could practise visualisation for a few weeks before you attempt the exercise again.

Sometimes, however, it is not our approach and it is the system. If we have created such a rigid picture of ourselves that we struggle to overcome the mistakes from our past, occasionally we need to supplement loving ourselves with other activities in order to loosen the negative perceptions sufficiently to face them fairly. If our conditioning has been so strong that the negative view we have of ourselves combines with our understanding of the world to validate them, then maybe we need to look at these key areas closer. The most practical course of action is to identify the key times in our life from where we have formed opinions of our self identity and look at them with a loving approach to identify what in our interpretation of these events is fact and what is perception. If we can recognise these misconceptions and remove them, then we can re-examine our understanding of these key moments in our life. As we begin to understand the blips that exist in our self portrait, we become better informed, allowing us to make an informed decision on what is forgivable and what isn't.

One technique available to help us look closer at our history and assist us in understanding how we got to where we are, is known as the timeline technique. The timeline technique is a process of setting a timeline out in front of you, a line representing your life, and making notes of specific times in your history relevant to the exercise. This process of making notes in relation to whatever we feel is significant, allows us to get a clearer understanding of our own evolution.

If you want to create your own time line I suggest that you get yourself a large page (or two), a few different coloured pens or pencils, (or even crayons or paints!) and if possible get yourself a ruler or a device to draw straight lines and divide them up. You can also do this free hand! Turning your page to landscape, draw three lines from left to right, starting about an inch in and ending about an inch short of the edge, and space them equally top to bottom with sufficient space above and below them. Add a few years to your age in order to have a number devisable by three, and then divide by three. I added one year onto my age to reach thirty six and then divided by three giving me twelve. Then I marked the first line from 0 to 12, the second from 12 to 24, and the third from 24 to 36. Apply your own figures like this so that you end up with three lines, allowing you to put a zero at the start of the first line and your last number at the end of the third line. Finish off by dividing each line into equal sections, with small ticks on the timeline to represent each specific year.

The timeline activity will take a significant period of time and it is something that works best if you come back to it on a few occasions. As a result of this, you will benefit from it most if you take your time. The purpose of this time line is to allow us to look back over our lives with clarity and make note of the memories we have that seem significant. It will allow us to understand the difference in events and experiences and ultimately help us understand the discrepancy between truths and inferences. When we have completed our time line, we will be able to identify the obstacles which exist that block off our ability to love and forgive ourselves and trace them back to their (ultimately forgivable) roots. You will benefit immensely from having as complete a timeline as possible before you start to break it down.

I would like to make you aware of what might happen throughout the course of this exercise. When we start to look at why the significant events in our past occurred and what we took from them, we will inevitably uncover other memories that we had previously allowed to drift away. For some people the penny might drop quickly when they can easily see how the mistakes they made came about and how they are truly forgivable, but for others this might become distressing as they uncover memories which feel uncomfortable. If this is you, please take a step back and take some time to compose yourself. You might want to reread chapter six to help prepare yourself for mistakes you made or situations you were a party to.

If you feel overwhelmed at any stage, then you should contemplate stopping. Maybe you might like to take time to have a chat with someone you trust or a health professional. It might seem like a massive step to talk to someone, but you would be surprised by the strength you can gain by doing so. There is no time limit on how long this process should take. Indeed, you should remember that you will have spent many years and possibly even a few decades to get to where you are now, and you aren't going to change things holistically over night!

The best way to approach this is to let what is in your head just spill out onto the page, letting your memories dictate the pattern. With your page in front of you, just start remembering anything significant events in your past and make a quick note of why they are significant. Don't be afraid to make brief notes on what you feel, and don't be afraid to jump from age four to forty! This is simply about pouring our self perception onto a page.

Don't try to push this exercise or put rules to it. Write as much as you can when you can, and come back to it whenever you have something to write. Make an effort but don't force yourself. Try to come back to it five or six times over a two week period and just keep filling in little significant memories. There will probably be a few things on your time line that you feel uncomfortable about. That is OK. When you have filled your time line out to a level you feel happy with, we have finished part one.

For part two I would like you to copy the following text onto a bit of card. *We are where we are in life as a direct result of the choices we have made, including choosing not to make a decision, and every choice we make is aimed to be the best choice for us personally based upon the belief system, value, experience and knowledge we posses.* Also, it would help you if you had three coloured pens or pencils.

Look at all the memories that you have noted down and circle them to signify three different groups. Colour one should signify happy memories. Your second colour should be used to circle memories where you did something wrong. The third colour is used for times when you were sad as a result of how you perceived people thought of or acted towards you. Take your time to do this as most memories will have overlapping emotions. Sometimes you will have a happy memory and you might have a feeling of sadness attached to it. Memories are intricate, but they are also relative to the state you are in when you access them.

Next, starting at the beginning of your line, find the first instance where you have signified a mistake that you have made. Let yourself relax and visualise the memory for a time. Take a mental walk around the situation and try to make sense of what it is you have a problem with, and then recite out loud the text you copied on the card. If you find it helps, try to imagine yourself feeling love and forgiveness towards the younger more vulnerable you, whilst explaining why everything is ultimately forgivable.

When you have read this out, trace the causes of what led to the conflict in feelings and attempt to forgive that which led to the mistake. Allow yourself to feel grateful for the fact that you are a good enough individual to face the mistakes you have made in order to redress them in whatever way you choose.

When you do this, let yourself appreciate what you feel and let your thoughts dictate what you do next. Has there been a shift in your feelings towards yourself? Is this something that might require revisiting? Hopefully you will want to go to the next relevant memory and work to understand and forgive the mistakes you have made. You might, however, decide to take your time over this and this too is OK, as long as you don't use it as a means to avoid.

Return to this exercise over days and weeks and each time you look at a mistake read the text to remind yourself how you got to the point of the mistake. Give yourself the credit you deserve and make the decisions your thoughts require of you. When you feel like it, move to the happier memories or the memories where your sadness was as a result of the perceived thoughts or actions of others and again apply the text. This should allow you to begin to forgive yourself and some, if not all, of those who have affected you. This ability to forgive is worthy of gratitude, so feel love for yourself and for all the good things you are party to.

While doing this, we should also take a little 'me time' to practise all the elements of the first exercise. This journey of appreciation and forgiveness requires that we allow ourselves to build up a reserve of good feelings to make sure we are strong enough to meet anything head on. These self evaluations can be like ghosts we are afraid of until we confront them. There is no fixed method or time line that you must adhere to. The important thing is that you apply yourself properly and put the effort in, and that you leave fear to the side.

Uri Geller was once on a radio station I listen to in

Ireland called Today FM. Most people in the UK and Ireland know of Uri through his television profile and the wider world might recognise him through his friendship with a certain deceased megastar. Anyway, Uri is one of these guys who for years had performed and carried mystical feats which ranged from the bending of spoons to the missing of penalties in a televised international soccer match. Uri is met with various perceptions depending upon what you actually believe, but there is one thing for certain in my mind: Uri loves to love. In this specific interview, he used the phrase "attitude of gratitude." The reason I mention Uri is two fold. Firstly, it is very easy to laugh at or judge someone who you don't understand. The joke or judgement often says more about your vulnerabilities than those of the figure of ridicule. Secondly, I would like to say thank you to him for bringing that simple saying to so many people.

Attempting to have an attitude of gratitude is a great way to accessing a loving feeling within us. Being grateful for things like flowers and smells and colours, or chocolate or our loved ones is an amazing feeling. Simply being grateful for our ability to recognise these beautiful things which surround us is an amazing thing. All these things which you can be grateful for can benefit you by assisting in the promotion of love and wisdom from within.

Finally, moving from the topic of learning techniques

onto how to love ourselves, I have one last offering which is my own daily routine. As a child and teenager, I used to wake up every morning and pray to God and the angels and saints. I used to recite specific prayers that I had learned by heart, and then I would thank God for certain things and ask him for other things. Praying has a wonderful way of focusing and galvanising us. Although I was happy to pray, I managed to feel judged even by God, as I guessed he knew my thoughts before I knew them. Eventually I prayed only through repetition or repentance.

Nowadays, I wake up and do two breathing exercises as I give thanks and love to myself and everyone around me. Firstly, I get out of my bed and sit upright and begin the first exercise. I breath in for eight and out for four, for about five or ten minutes. As I do this I think about my life and give thanks for all that exists and I give thanks to myself for seeing and feeling and wanting to preserve all that I love. I thank myself for having the strength and desire to have love in my heart and live through the wisdom of love. I then focus and nudge myself towards the day ahead by thinking of plans I might employ to get the best out of myself. I end my routine with an exercise similar to one known as fire-breathing, were you breathe very quickly (three to four short breaths per second) through your nose. I do this for a few minutes clearing my head before committing myself to approaching my day as efficiently as possible, with the underlying goal of maintaining the feeling of love inside me, looking for opportunities for enriching my happiness.

At night time, before I go to bed, I do the second exercise first whilst thinking about the day that I just had, giving thanks to myself and anyone I interacted with. After five minutes of this I do a version of the first of my morning breathing exercises, where I change the lengths of breaths to in for four and out for eight. As I clear my head I allow thoughts of gratitude to flow in. I thank myself for making the effort to feel gratitude and love for myself. I thank others for the part they play in my life, and I forgive myself and others for the actions they have done to get me down. When I feel I have finished with each occasion, I gradually allow myself to simply feel love for myself. Still breathing in for four and out for eight, I maintain my feeling of love inside me and I 'put my day to bed.' Then I happily fall asleep.

MAKING SENSE OF OUR WORLD

It is my belief that a large proportion of people who live in Europe and America are judgemental as a result of their socialisation, and this trait has become debilitating. We have been conditioned to quickly generalise to sum people up, as a life mechanism, to make a judgement on them based upon the information at hand. This approach harks back to a time when life was simpler, when communication and education lacked in sufficient depth and when our perceptions of ourselves were shaped by religions. Generalising, an approach to learning which is immensely practical, was a simple answer for a simple time. To be judgemental can be defined as being of the inclination to pass judgement on someone without full appreciation of the other person's reasoning.

As society evolved, the art of generalising has become more and more misused over time. Gone were the simplicities of what we were looking to explain or understand, and in its place came inadequate responses to questions which grew in their complexity. The art of being judgemental was often encouraged by those who held uneducated opinions or those who felt the need to repress others. In the last millennium, society had been dangerously judgemental in areas of gender, race, creed, colour, age and physicality and unfortunately in some instances these wrong doings have not yet been eradicated.

There is a bridge between informed generalising and being judgemental. Making an informed generalisation is about putting together related facts and transferring the message of what they are saying. If we eat too much sugar or fat based foods it will lead to an unhealthy diet which can ultimately affect our health, so an informed generalisation would be to say too much fatty food is bad for us. It would, however, be judgemental to say that someone who appears to be overweight is so because they eat too much or that they must deserve to be obese as they should know better.

As a society, we are conditioned to be judgemental of others, to put our reasoning onto the actions of others in order to explain them. We are taught to make sense of the world through interpreting external events using our personal experiences and values, attributing reasons to the actions of others. As in happiness, the process of passing judgements is directly related to the mindset we were in when we ask a question which creates the need for a generalisation. Did person 'A' carry out an action towards person 'B' because they were jealous or was it a mistake? Did Person 'X' spill my drink on purpose or not?" If we are happy we generally look for a positive explanation, but if we are unhappy or have an issue, the outcome will be affected by negative attribution. As with happiness, if we can interpret the same events differently depending upon our mood, relationship or knowledge of any persons involved, we are constantly at risk of making errors that might have consequences to ourselves. By being judgemental we can cause ourselves unnecessary stress when we attribute sentiment to actions incorrectly, like when 'she did that because she doesn't like me'. In scenarios like this, even when the judgment is correct, the assumption is not beneficial. I feel that most of us have become judgemental because of the quirk in social evolution mentioned in an earlier chapter and this has led us to evaluate ourselves through the eyes of others.

Being influenced as a result of our perception of how others might view us, can seriously affect how we act. Sometimes we hide from challenging ourselves because we are afraid of looking silly. Failure can be bad enough, but painting a picture of how we might be viewed either generally or as the result of a specific event, can produce a horrific picture in our minds. We can limit our levels of interaction with the world around us simply because we are being judgemental of the opinions of others towards us, causing fear. Some people can go the other way and use this as a motivational tool, doing things in spite of what people think but this too is flawed, even if it produces some successful outcomes. I would suggest that either way, what other people think should only ever be secondary to what we feel. We should not empower the perceived wisdom of others or restrict ourselves based on these views as nobody knows us like we know ourselves.

How I believed people perceived me was a very important factor for most of my life. It wasn't until I became comfortable with loving myself that I realised how much I had been restricted by it.

When I first started to write this book a few years ago, my intentions were to write down my theory, explain it and then apply it to everything I could. I wanted to strip life down and empower people to strip away the things which I believed restricted them.

Everywhere I looked I was starting to see how the world we live in was contaminated by externalism and judgementalism. I wanted to write a book that looked at five or ten of the largest maladies of modern living with a view to explaining them chapter by chapter, in the hope that I could maybe speed up the salvation of the world. In short, I just wanted to fix things. However, as I started living my theory, committing myself to making the effort to love myself even when I was finding the whole thing difficult, the book that I thought I was going to write became a different animal. In simply reminding myself to love myself every day and feel grateful for the smaller things every day and trying to find opportunities for being loving and loving myself; I have changed and so has my book.

My intention all that time ago was to create a tool to help people who were sad, to understand how close at hand happiness can be. I wanted to help people who felt depressed; especially those who hadn't really spoken to anyone about it. I wanted to help them to gather enough strength to take the first step. I wanted to create a tool for people who were bullied, people with eating disorders, people with addictions, people with low self esteem, people who were being excluded by the rules of society and those who contemplated taking their own life. I wanted to help anyone who had pain in their lives to see where that pain had come from. The simplicity of the whole theory has meant that this is not necessary.

It is not for me to try to tell you how to see your world. I have put enough thoughts into your head by describing how I got to my theory, and it is important that I don't lose track of myself and grey the line between my opinion and the theory of loving yourself first. I changed my approach to this book because as I became more able to love myself I started to understand more and more of what the theory has to offer.

Instead of me attempting to do justice to important topics like those mentioned above, topics that I believe need to be approached with a higher level of understanding than presently exists, I looked at my understanding of these issues from a different direction. What follows is a result of simply applying the wisdom of love to how I see the problems of the world.

Imagine you were fully competent at loving yourself. Imagine that you were able to get up in the morning and feel grateful for the chance to live another day with all that might be on offer. Imagine knowing that no matter what the random nature of the world might throw at you, that you know you are strong enough to deal with it and will enjoy it no matter what. Imagine feeling so strong and safe that almost nothing could cause you to be afraid.

Now imagine living as that person within the confines of your normal life, strong and loving. Would you feel sufficiently affected by the opinions of others? Would they be able to make you feel bad about yourself? No, because you would realise that anyone who is trying to force their opinion on you doesn't fully understand you, or that they have issues of their own that they have not yet dealt with. Would you feel inclined to judge or be judged in terms of looks or fashion? Probably not. Would you feel so unhappy with your body that you wanted to starve it? Would you feel the need for intermittent happiness and develop an addiction? Would you feel sad about yourself? Would you bully someone? Would you overeat out of comfort? Would you feel so low that you would seriously take your own life? Would you judge another?

I am not suggesting that loving yourself is an answer that should be foisted onto everyone as the only solution to everything. However, I have yet to come across something that cannot be, at the very least, made less painful through the process of loving yourself. Think of any social, personal or global problem there is and then think how it might be affected if the people involved all tried to love themselves. Would the problem get better or worse? Would resources be wasted? Would lives be saved?

I have an opinion which I would like to test in the future, but as of today it is completely untested. My opinion is that if we were all shown how to love ourselves unconditionally, through example, simply and holistically in schools and in our homes, we would be less susceptible to the problems that blight our societies. I believe that most problems can be at worst eased, at best irradiated by loving yourself. Would you be depressed if you loved yourself? Would you want to give up on the possibilities of life if you loved yourself? Would you compare yourself unfavourably to manufactured stereotypes, would you allow yourself to support these stereotypes? Would you self harm or starve yourself if you loved yourself?

The answers to these questions will always be your own answers, and the strength to take the first step is often the biggest restriction we have, but it is only a relative restriction. If you are sad and you would like to be happier, what have you got to lose by attempting to love yourself and putting in a bit of effort? Remember, it is not what happens but how you view what has occurred that affects how you feel, and the happier you are, the happier you will perceive what you see.

It is not about magic potions or ten steps to happiness. It is not about wishing your life away chasing a 'secret' or following some cosmic ordering. It is not about waiting for life to affect you. It is about accepting who you are, how you got to where you are, and deciding what you need to do next. It is about ceasing to blame and to judge, no longer feeling hard done by, even when you have suffered all the woes in the world, and making a decision to give yourself the chance to see what happiness might be like. Stop trying to change yourself into someone you think other people might value. Instead, love yourself and let *you* be the judge of who you are.

Practise loving yourself. You create habits over time, and love is something that needs to be practised in order to get the best out of it. Don't begrudge this effort because this can only be in response to a limiting belief you hold.

Instead, understand that effort is directly related to what you really get out of your life. Any barrier you are putting up to stop you facing the parts of yourself that you don't like is one created by the fear of judgement. It is these parts that require your own forgiveness.

What other options do you have? Should you dream your life away in the hope that you might be the lucky one in twenty million who wins a sum of money that will probably create more issues than it solves? Do you forget yourself and dream so much that you forget to live? Is it a good use of your time being angry with the poor cards you were dealt? The answer is yours, it is your choice. You'll benefit from making a decision and choosing what action you should take, remembering the fact that you are always happier when you feel unconditional love. At least then, if you find yourself in a position where you are not happy with where you are, you can look back and see where you went right or wrong. If all else fails at least you lived.

Be; life is best appreciated from a happy perspective so if you want to be happy, know your options. Realise that when you dream about what you want, like the house, car and success that most self help books thrust you towards, you are simply creating representations of the emotions you want to feel. Understand that these emotions you want to feel may require a little hard work or a bit more effort.

Don't let others dictate as to how you achieve these emotions and ultimately you will be able to achieve them in your own way.

Make a choice. In doing so you are choosing the direction your life will take. If you aren't ready to choose a definitive direction, choose to delay making a choice; it gives you back control. Make choices. If you simply drift through life, it might turn out good or it might turn out bad, but you'll always be at the behest of the elements. If you make decisions you will have ownership of the reasons for, and the outcomes of, each decision. If you make a mistake, it is easy to forgive yourself.

Exercise and eat well. There is no getting away from it. Exercise is important and so is diet. The better your diet the less energy your body will waste dealing with toxins. Maintaining a sufficient level of exercise helps your body create the chemicals we need to stay balanced. Alcohol, cigarettes, drugs, fast food and other processed foods put our bodies under stress. You can love yourself even if you live an unhealthy life but you will be more capable of grasping the opportunities out there if you look after yourself.

Most problems in the world are caused by 'ego'. Ego is caused by learning to value yourself against what others might think of you. Valuing yourself against what others might think of you is the road to unhappiness. Your ego distracts you and plays with your mind. It is that 'he said, she said', 'he has, she has' thing. Valuing yourself in relation to what you perceive others hold in high regard is ultimately a sliding scale of which you have no control.

Everyone is different and most of us are making it up as we go along. If we try to live by moral or religious standards that we don't fully believe in, we will eventually throw the baby out with the bath water. Your faith or belief system does not need to define you. You define you. Don't be afraid to question your own beliefs and don't waste time trying to convert others to yours. Live your life by the values you believe in, and if you do this with love, it is impossible to go wrong.

Depression, when not clinical, is a slowly evolved belief system caused by someone thinking they are not worth as much as someone else. If you are depressed, try loving yourself: you really have little to lose. If you know someone who is depressed, don't simply try and make them feel good about themselves: you can become a crutch to their malady. Go further, show yourself love and you will exude enough love to give them the strength to love themselves. Support them to deal with their depression and create the strategies that will never find them on their own.

Don't do things just because someone else does, because if you are wrong you won't know why. Don't be afraid of choosing the wrong option; make sure you learn something from your decision.

And finally, when you are dealing with children you should always remember who the kid is and who the adult is. Children should be seen, heard, loved and nurtured but they should also be allowed the freedom of being children. They are rarely young adults, and even when they are, what is it you like about young adults that is better than being a child. If you have children then don't raise them in a particular manner simply because that was how you were raised, remember, your parents will have made plenty of mistakes and life has moved on. Love yourself and think about the impact of love on their lives. Make the effort to give them time and help them to learn. Most importantly show them the difference in being right and wrong in relation to your values, differentiate between punishment and consequence. Show them that you love them and yourself unconditionally.

There is nothing in this whole world which cannot be made better, no question that cannot be made clearer, no wrong that cannot be righted, when you learn to love yourself unconditionally.

LOVE YOURSELF FIRST

My theory is simple. There is no 'secret of life'. The key to happiness is to love yourself unconditionally.

If we are happy, the world usually seems like a good place to live, but if we feel sad it can become very challenging indeed. If we are generally happy people, we are less affected by the negativities of the world. However, if our happiness relies on the happiness of others or the simplicity of situations, we will always be vulnerable to someone else's unhappiness or the random events of the world.

In order to be truly happy we need to love ourselves first. If you love yourself, you will always have an inner happiness, because loving yourself first allows you to be loving and forgiving, gracious and non-judgemental. If you have an inner happiness you will always find a relatively positive approach to even the most painful or negative of things. If you can react positively to the negativities of life, you will be less affected or distracted by them, leaving you free to be grateful and appreciative of the good things in life. Your general happiness will continue to grow if you keep loving yourself.

If we don't love ourselves first, we will have to receive love or love others in order to feel truly happy. This includes receiving love from God (s) and/or nature. If we rely upon receiving love to make us feel happy, our entire existence will be defined by our approach to giving love to or receiving love from others. We will place a value on ourselves based upon what we believe others think of us, of how deserving we may or may not be in relation to receiving love.

Because of the nature of not loving yourself, and the fact that we live in a society that doesn't encourage people to love themselves, the ability of someone else to love you cannot be consistent if they don't love themselves first. Therefore, someone else may not always be able to show their love for you when you require it, meaning that even when you believe you are deserving of love, you are not guaranteed to receive it. And then love becomes conditional. Conditional love is judgemental and specific to the opinions of both the giver and the receiver. Conditional love, over time, can become brittle and its nature can be its main weakness being that it can be viewed very differently by both the giving and the receiving parties.

If we learn to love ourselves first, we always have access to love and as such we will always have access to happiness.

If we live our life loving ourselves, we will always strive to be the best 'us' we can be and bit by bit, loving ourselves first will eventually lead to having the strength to allow us to achieve anything we truly want.

We can walk to the ends of the earth, chase lost civilisations and devise new God's. We can war against each other, covet resources and manipulate global events. I can devote my life to fixing people to live my way and never truly be successful, or I can learn to love myself and live my own life to the best of my ability. Loving yourself is so simple; it has been over-looked since the beginning of time.

Lightning Source UK Ltd.
Milton Keynes UK
UKOW042315280912

199827UK00003B/2/P